I0425606

SELF-DISCIPLINE TO CHANGE YOUR LIFE:

Develop Self-Control, Willpower, Mental Toughness, and the Ability to Achieve Your Goals

Robert Hensley

Table of Contents

OTHER BOOKS BY ROBERT HENSLEY

Productivity Habits: Proven Techniques to Increase Personal Productivity and Achieve Goals (Time management and Productivity Series Book 1)

Stop Procrastinating: Simple Steps to Increase Productivity and Overcome Procrastination (Time Management and Productivity Series Book 2)

Change Your Habits Now: Effective Way to Transform Yourself and Change Life for Better (Small Changes for Happy Life Series Book 1)

Introduction

Self-discipline will teach you how to think and act with proper discernment.

Temptations, peer pressure, drowning in stress, and, of course, practicing bad habits, can all lead to making decisions that only cause more stress and temptations to cement into your life and thus lock you in a vicious circle that can feel like a prison. There is a key to free yourself from this prison of bad habits though, and that key has been in your hands all along. When you transform into a self-disciplined person, you will obtain mastery of the self.

The core of self-discipline is willpower. When your willpower is high, you can find that inner strength to keep going, especially when you feel like you can't go on anymore. In addition, willpower will help you find the means to get up and beat procrastination.

Mastery of self-discipline is imperative in order to get what you want out of life. You can improve your self-discipline even if you already know what it is and have relative control over your habits. Once you begin intentionally working on your discipline with purpose, you will find that you are able to get more goals accomplished each day without putting in any extra effort.

What is beneficial about greater self-discipline is that it has the ability to make you more naturally productive and efficient. Now, there will be some work involved with sustainably improving your level of discipline, but you will work on this over time, so you are sure to find that no step is too hard to overcome.

It is important that you do not just rely on your initial motivation to keep you going, since this is fleeting. Instead, you want to improve your self-discipline mindset. This makes it much easier to pursue your goals and ambitions in the long run than a temporary form of motivation can.

Now you will begin to answer the hard questions — remember, this will lay the groundwork for your mindset to become one that is naturally more self-disciplined, ready to deploy you towards your goals at a moment's notice.

When you harness your willpower and marshal your energies toward a specific goal, you enable yourself to achieve anything. This is, perhaps, the most important thing you can do to give yourself a push in the right direction.

It is time for you to start enjoying life in a bigger way by learning how to use your willpower and discipline as your greatest superpower against life. Learning how to use yourself as your greatest superpower leads to you being able to rely on yourself to get things done and accomplish everything you set out to achieve in life.

Self-discipline gives people the ability to become their own best weapon against life because they now have the capacity to control themselves in a very powerful manner. When you have mastered self-discipline, you go from being the type of person who has uncontrolled emotional responses to challenging situations to a person who can control their emotional responses.

After reading the content filled within the pages of this very book, you can expect to begin experiencing many incredible benefits from your shifts in life. You will start to experience an incredible level of inner strength and character, and the ability to withstand temptations in life.

This book aims to help you live your life in general in a more disciplined way. Discipline is not just for children; growing up and becoming adults does not automatically make them more disciplined. Discipline is not synonymous with punishment, punishment, or severity. It is possible for anyone to become a disciple of discipline.

Chapter 1: What is Self-discipline?

Self-discipline is the ability to say no to things you have developed a love for, in order to attain your goals in less time. Self-discipline is facing the strongest form of temptation and overcoming it.

Suppose you find yourself in a situation where someone very attractive tries to seduce you when you have made a vow to stay sex-free for a certain period of time. The ability to ignore the seductive moves of that stunning person is self-discipline.

Sometimes, self-discipline is the most complicated ability that a person can obtain or develop, because it includes organizing, responsibility, resisting external factors that can slow down progress, and, in all cases, sacrifice.

Self-discipline is the ability to know what is important and say "NO" to things that are less important, even though they are hard to resist.

Self-discipline is a learned behavior; no one is born self-disciplined. Like any other skill, self-discipline needs to be cultivated. It is the fruit that is yielded when we learn how to effectively challenge ourselves and experience the deeper inner potential that lies within us.

Self-discipline is the ability to resist immediate gratification and be undeterred by the bumps on the road while moving toward what you are trying to achieve.

As for developing self-discipline, a common response to why they have not developed greater self-discipline was that their lives were too busy and that they did not have enough time to develop it.

Self-discipline is the ability to be able to control your emotions and feelings to a point where it can help you overcome your weaknesses and desire to give into temptation. Self-discipline is a state of mind. It is something you can learn. Once cultivated, it becomes a part of who you are. You may wonder if this change is still possible. Yes, it absolutely is.

The road to self-discipline is going to put you to the test and push you beyond your comfort zone. However, it will also make you a much stronger and better person. There is a reason why we often hear successful individuals attribute their success to hard work and self-discipline.

Chapter 2: Causes of Lack of Self-Discipline

It is wrong for you to think that self-discipline is an inborn trait. Such erroneous thoughts will make you believe you can't possibly build self-discipline if you lack it. No one is born with self-discipline. If you want to become self-disciplined, you can do so with the right determination and commitment. However, a number of factors could be responsible for your lack of self-discipline or your inability to build or develop self-discipline.

Here are some of the common causes of lack of self-discipline in most people today:

Lack of Purpose

The purpose is what you live for. It's that one driving force that keeps you going. The purpose is that very thing you remember and makes you decide to keep on moving on, no matter the level of discouragement you encounter.

When you lack purpose, it is not possible for you to be self-disciplined. One man once said that the purpose of life was to have a life of purpose, and I quite agree with him. A life without purpose is not worth living, because a person that has nothing to live for has never truly lived.

Lack of Goals

This one is closely related to the lack of purpose mentioned above. Your goal at any point in your life is like a compass that tells you where you are going and the right path to take in order to get there.

Negative Influences

A number of factors determine your dominant habits and character traits. One major thing that contributes to shaping your beliefs and your character is the environment you spend more time in than anywhere else. If you grow up in volatile suburbs, where crime is a normal thing and getting involved in certain criminal activities is nothing to be ashamed of, it would be extremely difficult to become self-disciplined.

If you are unlucky to grow up in an environment where there are no laws and everything goes, you may not see reasons to become self-disciplined early in life. Another such strong factor is the company you keep. If you hang out with people whose watchword is indiscipline, it will take a miracle for you to be self-disciplined without breaking away from such a company.

Negative Stereotypes

To some people, it is not possible for them to become self-disciplined because they believe they were born to break every breakable rule. But in reality, anyone can overcome indiscipline and become self-disciplined by making certain changes in lifestyle and habit changes.

Lack of Willpower

Most people lack adequate willpower to enable them effect the needed positive changes in their habits and lifestyles in order to become more successful and productive. People who lack willpower do not even attempt to change things that are negative in their lives, even when they do, they cannot persevere after an initial setback or failure.

Fear of Failure

Fear is one of the most dangerous enemies. It won't let you fulfill anything in life and is often one of your first barriers. But it's necessary to overcome fear. If we don't, we get stuck in our actual situation with no probability of personal, professional, academic, or any other type of growth.

Today's Decaying Culture

We have come to the point where the very fabric of good morals is being eroded at a fast rate. A society whose values, cultures, and traditions are dying speedily can only produce individuals with every trace of moral decadence. If you live in a society where people no longer frown at what used to be seen as an abnormality a few years ago, that could be a reason for your lack of self-discipline.

The Media

We are in the Internet age, and we have our own ways of doing things. The media have contributed to the decay in people's character, which has made people lose their self-discipline. The way the media hype and promote habits that should be a thing of worry and concern to society makes it more difficult for self-discipline to be instilled. Imagine trying to quit your addiction to starchy foods, sugary foods, and all other junk that makes you fat, and the media keep telling you why you can't do without these unhealthy foods.

Excuse Lifestyle

Self-discipline includes a non-excuse lifestyle. Many people adopted the habit of always having excuses for the mistakes made. First of all, as adults, we have to accept our errors and face the consequences as a deserved punishment. It's a necessary process that will heighten our capability of improving.

Having Too Many Goals

There's nothing more dangerous for self-discipline than having too many things to do or wanting to reach too many goals. This lifestyle is going to totally defocus your efforts to develop your self-discipline. If you don't take your time to prioritize and select the things you really want to do, you will end up with a lot of things to do and with no time to complete them. That's why it is very important to have chosen the most important objectives to achieve, so you can focus completely on them.

Lack of Self-Esteem

You must know that you are able to accomplish any task you propose. If you are often underestimating yourself and repeating yourself you won't be able to perform anything or something specific, you probably won't. Lack of self-esteem is a very recurrent problem nowadays, especially in this globalized world, where talent and competition are everywhere. Many people fall into a depression when they go to work on something and realize that there are a lot of people who also do the same thing way better and have more experience.

The Weak State of Health

This is a very important factor when evaluating your lack of self-discipline. Having very good mental and physical health will help you build self-discipline. The lack of sleep, malnourishment, not having lunch at adequate times, and any other bad alimentary habit will keep you weak and unfocused.

Distraction

This is a very pleasant cause for the lack of self-discipline. We'd like to do an activity, but suddenly, we want to have something to eat, we want to take a break or a nap, we'd like to watch a movie, the Internet is demanding my attention, someone's commented on my Facebook wall, and then, time goes by, and we have lost the entire day. Distraction is a very common factor that carries us away from being self-disciplined. It might be one of the worst, because this temptation will always be with us, and things or events that can distract us are going to be available all the time.

Chapter 3: Common Habits That Show You Lack Self-Discipline

Sexual Promiscuity

Everyone loves sex, but when it becomes the most important part of your life, abuse sets in. If you find yourself engaging in unhealthy sexual habits such as sleeping around with many different sex partners; having sex without protection even when you know the dangers it exposes you and others to; engaging in sex for money, no matter how hard the economic crunch has hit you; and/or engaging in sexual acts in public places such as clubs, public parks, amusement parks, alleys, lobbies, shopping malls, parking lots, school premises, classrooms, offices, toilets, etc. If you find yourself unable to keep your sexual urges under control to the point that you throw all decency and decorum to the winds, know you need to do something to increase your level of self-discipline.

Drunkenness

If you find yourself in love with alcohol to the point that you place it above everything else, it is a good sign you are not disciplined. No one is saying you should not drink alcohol; the point is that you should apply moderation in everything you do. Know the level of alcohol your system reacts to and the level of alcohol that can make your system lose control of its normal functions and behaviors. Keep in mind those levels and do not go over that limit. If you find yourself longing for alcohol more than you long to become a better or a more successful person, then you must take urgent steps to address the issue before it gets out of hand.

Laziness

This one is among the major signs of indiscipline you can find in any individual. If you are self-disciplined, you will find it difficult to hold on to your bed when others are out there looking for how to make ends meet. A disciplined person knows when to jump out of bed, get dressed, roll up their sleeves, and get to work. If you find yourself lazing about when you should either be studying or working, then you need to help yourself before the world leaves you behind.

Procrastination

This one goes hand-in-hand with laziness. If you are lazy, the next thing for you to do is to put everything away until a later and a more convenient time. If you find yourself procrastinating and leaving everything until a later time, you lack self-discipline. People with self-discipline understand the importance of starting every task on time and staying put until they have accomplished it. Procrastination is one of the reasons why indiscipline has remained a vice that has robbed many of their once-bright destinies. Whenever you find yourself leaving until tomorrow what you can conveniently begin or accomplish today, it shows that you lack self-discipline.

Cheating

If you cheat, you lack self-discipline, and there will always be a limit to what you can achieve in life. No one has ever recorded success on anything in life while cutting corners.

Cutting corners might actually get you there fast, but in reality, it will always get you off the top faster than it got you there.

Impatience

If you are fond of trying to rush things when they require a little patience for perfection to be achieved, you lack self-discipline, and you can hardly get anything done with perfection.

Lack of Diligence

Have you seen a person diligent in their work? That man has self-discipline. It is common to experience challenges in your line of work or business. Even if you are still studying, there comes a time when you experience unusual setbacks that require you to be diligent and persevere. If you are self-disciplined, you will see obstacles as opportunities to work harder to come out with a better result than you were working towards.

Selfishness

Selfish people are not self-disciplined. If you are always thinking about your own good, even when it is to the detriment of everyone else, it shows you need to sharpen your self-discipline more. Selfishness is one thing that can give you instant gratification but will hurt you in the long run. It is a self-discipline that helps you share what you have with others.

Gluttony

Greed is also a common bad habit that shows you lack self-discipline. Gluttony and greed are the same concepts focused on different objectives. Gluttony is often related to food and greed to possessions and success. A greedy person is never going to be self-disciplined due to the consequences it has, and this can be illustrated in several ways.

Chapter 4: What You Lose Due to Your Lack of Self-Discipline

Juicy Business Opportunities

The same way your level of discipline is visible for all to see, your lack of self-discipline is equally obvious, if not more conspicuous. So when you lack self-discipline, no one wants to go into business with you. Most people who lack self-discipline are always bypassed when it comes to choosing people for a vital assignment. Your inability to keep your gluttony, drunkenness, anger, malice, envy, and all other such vices under check can make you lose juicy opportunities that could change the entire course of your life for the better.

Healthy Relationships

If you take time to study why many relationships and marriages fail, you will be surprised to discover that the majority of failed relationships and marriages crumbled because someone could not control an addiction. What are the major reasons for people breaking up? Issues such as infidelity, physical abuse, verbal abuse, sexual abuse, addiction to drugs or alcohol, laziness, uncaring attitude, and several others are the major culprits.

Respect from People around You

I have never seen any well-respected man or woman who lacks self-discipline, and neither have I seen a person without self-discipline who commands respect. Once you are not able to deal with your lack of self-discipline, you stand the risk of losing respect from people around you. When you lack self-discipline, even your own kids won't respect you. Without self-discipline, your closest friends and family members won't hold you in high esteem, because you are prone to bring them shame, disgrace, and ridicule without warning.

Your Success

Self-discipline helps you manage your money better, manage your time better, manage your employees better, make more informed choices, treat every one of your employees fairly and equally, get your priorities right, follow changes in market trends, and influence all other factors that can affect your career or business. One mistake most successful people who lack self-discipline make is that they rest on their laurels because they believe they have arrived and cannot go back down.

Your Credibility

When you lack self-discipline, no one will believe you are up to any good. Even the areas where you could be an expert will suffer, because they will be overshadowed by your obvious lack of self-discipline. Everyone tends to avoid dealing with you when you lack self-discipline, because dealing with you would be tantamount to exposing themselves to risk.

Chapter 5: Benefits of Self-Discipline

Achieve More in Less Time

Most of the things you spend your time doing when you lack self-discipline add nothing towards the actualization of your goals. Most people have several duties they have to accomplish a day. As long as they are organized to fulfill those daily goals, they will be able to do it, avoiding procrastination.

Self-discipline makes you a better time manager. If you understand the great role effective time management plays on your overall success and wellbeing in life, you will do whatever it takes to become self-disciplined. Self-discipline enables you to know what time should be allocated to what task and when to back out of something that is preventing you from doing more important things. Self-discipline helps you realize you can channel the time you waste in nightclubs, bars, game houses, strip clubs, and all other such places where you get temporary gratification to more important things like drafting the plans towards your goal actualization. Self-discipline enables you to know when to stop planning and start acting.

Increase Your Confidence

Confidence is also a secondary effect from being self-disciplined, for it is a door which opens a new world: a world of your real abilities and skills. You might be a person who has not practiced well self-discipline, but you are very confident about what you're able to do. This means you have self-esteem; nevertheless, this feeling about being proud of yourself is related to your personality and can be dangerous if it is exaggerated.

Stay Focused

Staying focused on things that really matter not only applies to those people who try to mislead you so that you don't reach your goals, but also applies to yourself. It is very common this kind of situations, and it does not only happen with Facebook. Many social networks make you get carried away from doing the simplest tasks in your daily routine, so staying focused implies avoiding people who don't contribute to your objectives and instead desire to do non-productive things during the day.

Set Your Priorities Right

Once self-discipline sets in your life, your ability to think about your objectives and goals increases. Once you stay focused on your goals, you will be able to make a meaningful relationship between them and short-term activities. You will be able to define which tasks or activities are more important to the achievement and then, a selection process unfolds in order to reject those things that only subtract time and do not contribute to an improvement.

Develop Better, More Fulfilling Relationships

Self-disciplined people do not just do well professionally but also enjoy more meaningful, rewarding, and fulfilling relationships. When you are able to demonstrate discipline and maintain promises you've made to yourself, you are likelier to do the same with other people. Self-disciplined people are likelier to maintain their promises and commitment, while also influencing other people in a more positive way. When you display endless reserves of self-discipline, you boost the trust people place on you and come across as an individual with high integrity and responsibility. Developing high self-control means you are the master of your words, thoughts, and actions. This helps avoid conflicts and build more positive and less acrimonious relationships.

A relationship is a bond between people, and when they have reached a level of understanding each other, empathy becomes part of them. As in any relationship, each party is going to receive from the other, and commitment is essential in this. Self-disciplined people comprehend the importance of their friends and the necessity of not letting them down. They know when they are able to help or when it is necessary to say no.

Attain Your Goals

Self-discipline helps you attain your goals more easily in that you do not give in to factors that would want to frustrate you to the point where you surrender totally. With self-discipline, you get to the point where you can no longer heed the voice of discouragement and distractions. Self-discipline helps you endure harsh situations and pressures to get to the point where it could be said that you have successfully completed the task you have been working on. When you are self-disciplined, you will find distractions unattractive.

Build Determination

Self-discipline helps you go out of your way to do what most people won't dare in order to record success. Self-discipline sharpens the edges of your determination and teaches you not to accept no for an answer. It is self-discipline that helps you hold on and hang on to the last string when you have every reason to let go and call it quits.

Self-discipline gives you the courage to reach out on one limb in order to get to that fruit at the tip of the branch where anyone who tries to get to it risks a fatal fall.

Gain Self-Control

Self-control is always related to people with great willpower. In order to develop self-control there's another value we need to take into account: consciousness. We all are adults, and we have the ability to know the difference between good from the bad. Willpower consists of being conscious of and accepting the fact that, most of the time, those things you have come to love so much will have to wait until those short-term plans have been completed.

Become More Successful

That self-discipline is a prerequisite for true success in life is no longer news. No matter how good you are at what you do and how unparalleled your talents are, you will never attain the real height of success if you lack the adequate level of self-discipline to choose what really matters. Look at all the successful people you hear or read about all over the world today, and you will discover they all have one vital trait in common, and that trait is self-discipline.

Live an Empowered Life

Self-discipline also empowers you. When you know you have the ability to achieve whatever you set your eyes on, you stop settling for mediocre things and instead strive for excellence. Naturally, when you pursue excellence, your life becomes more empowered and meaningful.

Become More Productive

Self-discipline helps you forget how many times you have failed on that particular venture and keep trying until you arrive on Success Avenue. Self-discipline enables you to understand that there could be different ways of doing a particular thing, which inspires you to keep changing strategies until you find one that works perfectly for you.

Your level of self-discipline determines how productive you can be, both in your private business and as an employee. When you are self-disciplined, you won't mind working extra hours just to make sure you get the job done before closing for the day. When you are self-disciplined, you will be able to concentrate on learning better ways to get things done. Self-discipline makes you open to new ideas and knowledge. Self-discipline helps you achieve better results because you are disciplined enough to take responsibility for your mistakes and wrong choices.

Control More of Your Life

With self-discipline, you are in the driver's seat of your life. You are your own boss and cheerleader. You are able to turn in your work on time, establish your own goals and are seldom dominated by whims, moods, desires, short-term pleasures and negative or self-destructive habits. There is a reduced tendency to succumb to negative habits such as binge eating, addiction, inaction, and so on. You will not act like a victim of people, situations, and circumstances. Instead, you will hold the steering wheel of your thoughts, mindset, behavior, attitude, and actions.

Self-disciplined folks are likely to make less impulsive or rash decisions that can put them in troubled waters. They seldom act on momentary impulses, compelling desires, and short-term pleasures. Instead, their decisions and actions are almost always taken after considering the overall good in any situation. Since self-disciplined folks are wonderful at delaying pleasure or gratification and keeping their eyes on their larger picture, they rarely take hasty decisions that are later regretted. Making decisions in a composed, calm, analytical, and balanced way after considering all options and alternatives helps us make more rational, sensible, and balanced decisions.

Enhance Physical and Mental Health

What does a self-disciplined life include? It involves several things. This lifestyle includes healthy, balanced, and consistent habits like eating on a schedule, getting good sleep, following a regular exercise regime, and staying away from elements that are harmful to the body, mind, and spirit. This means that our body and mind are forever in top shape. In cases of illnesses and chronic ailments, sticking to a medicine schedule boosts your chances of feeling good. Likewise, following a disciplined schedule when it comes to consuming meals helps us stay fit, active, and healthy.

People who practice self-discipline as a way of life are more relaxed and enjoy a more fulfilling, balanced, and wholesome life that has everything from work to relaxing leisurely activities. Enjoyable activities aren't really fulfilling if they flow into their work time. These become more liabilities and guilt-inducing pursuits if they are done at the cost of your work, efficiency, and productivity.

Make the Right Choices

If you are self-disciplined, you will hardly make a wrong choice when it comes to choosing which vision to run with and which to lay aside. Self-discipline enables you to choose things that will still hold value for you, several years from now, and not things that will lose their validity and usefulness in no time at all. With self-discipline, you won't make choices based on sentiments and in pursuit of vain pleasures. Self-discipline enables you to separate the grains from the chaff when it comes to choosing what you spend your energy, time, and money pursuing.

Manage Money Better

People who lack self-discipline start spending their money as soon as they receive it without first planning how to spend it. Self-discipline teaches you to have a budget and stick to it. Self-discipline teaches you to pay yourself first before you pay anyone else at the end of every month.

Get More Organized

When you are self-disciplined, it will be easily seen in the way you do things. A self-disciplined person won't be caught living in a house where everything seems to be in disarray. A self-disciplined person won't be caught sitting in an office where papers are flying about in haphazard directions. Self-discipline enables you to organize your life in such a way that you can be able to see where you are getting things wrong and make necessary changes. When you are self-disciplined, you will be more organized, and when you are more organized, you will be more productive. And when you are more productive, success becomes your watchword.

Chapter 6: How to Build Self-Discipline

Building self-discipline is not as hard as your mind might have been conditioned to believe, though it will not come without some efforts and commitment. Here are some tested and trusted techniques you can adopt to help you build and maintain self-discipline.

Understand Where You Draw Inspiration from and What Turns Your Light Off

You have things that trigger your weaknesses and things that feed your major strengths. Discovering things that bring out the best in you and the things that bring your weakest points to the fore will go a long way toward building your self-discipline. This means you must commit some time to learn more about yourself. Building self-discipline boils down to overcoming your strongest negative urges, cravings, and desires.

Set a Goal

Every great achievement in life begins with setting a

feasible goal. By "feasible," I mean a goal that can be achieved within the deadline, all things being fair. In setting a goal to become more self-disciplined, you must put several factors into consideration, such as your most dominant traits, your habits, your major strengths, your weaknesses, things you have become addicted to, things you would want to change in your life, etc. Your goal should have a date for beginning your efforts to increase your level of self-discipline and a date by which you must have improved your level of self-discipline drastically.

Have a Plan

A goal might not be enough to take you to where you are going if you do not have a plan for how to get there. A goal tells you where you wish to go and when you wish to get there, but a plan helps you know the right path to take in order to arrive at your destination on time. Your plan should be detailed and tabulated. Your plan should involve daily activities you can engage in to help you become more self-disciplined.

Have Your Goal and Your Plan Written Down

Write down your goals and plans and place them where you can see them several times a day. You can post them on the walls of your room to enable you to get a glimpse of them the moment you rise in the morning and before you sleep at night. This constant reminding will help you keep the goal fresh and stay focused while on your self-discipline building project.

Start with Baby Steps

When it comes to how to build self-discipline, it is important to begin with simple baby steps you can easily learn to practice and move on to more complex steps as you record improvements. Building your self-discipline, like every other important lifestyle change in life, will not happen overnight.

Deny Yourself Certain Pleasures

Denying yourself certain pleasures will enable you to learn how to be in control of your life. It is all about practicing and mastering self-restraint. Force yourself to quit every old habit that hinders you from becoming a better you. Develop a deep hatred for things that distract you from pursuing your goals, such as TV addiction and excessive intake of drugs and alcohol. Holding on to any of these things that give you momentary pleasures will hinder you from amounting to anything meaningful in life. Find other ways to keep yourself occupied such as reading, working on a new business plan, volunteering in a community project, taking part in religious meetings, etc.

Get Rid of All Negative Habits

You can't be talking about becoming self-disciplined when you have not dealt with habits that are clear manifestations of your indiscipline. Getting rid of some negative habits won't be easy at all, because old habits die hard. However, with the right efforts and commitments, you can change any habit. One way to get rid of negative habits is to think about the habit thoroughly, weighing its benefits against its disadvantages. If possible, do some researches about that particular habit to enable you to get more facts about it, and then imagine what life could look like without those negative habits and find a constructive habit to replace the unconstructive habit.

Dump Your Negative Friends

The truth about self-discipline and the relationships you keep is that you can never become self-disciplined if you keep hanging out with the wrong crowd. If your circle of friends is made up of a bunch of undisciplined people, it will take a sort of a miracle for you to manage to have any self-discipline. Having friends who do not value self-discipline means you will always find yourself where negative behaviors are being exhibited. To build your self-discipline, it is important you get rid of friends that do not encourage you in your efforts to build discipline.

Change Environments

Nothing affects your habits and the habits of your children more than the environment you spend most of your daily time in. If you live in a city or district where good manners and habits have been thrown to the swine, it will be hard for you to cultivate any good habits toward becoming more self-disciplined. If you want to become a more self-disciplined person, perhaps you could start considering moving to a new home. Find a better neighborhood where people still have enough conscience not to engage in stomach-churning behaviors. Change your church, school, gym, etc., to help you meet people who value good morals and positive habits like you do.

Adopt New Daily Habits

Daily good habits are an excellent start to build self-discipline. Runners, for example, have to wake up every day, have breakfast on time, and go jogging at a specific time for a pre-defined amount of time. You can, with enough willpower, create good habits.

Persevere

Don't make the mistake of thinking you are now disciplined because you have been able to deal with bad habits such as addictions to harmful drugs and alcohol, overfeeding, arrogance, financial recklessness, infidelity, insincerity, etc. Some of these old habits will often want to return to you after a while. Whenever you fall into any of these ditched habits as a result of momentary weakness, you must make sure you get up and keep moving without looking back. Falling is normal on any success journey — it is staying down that makes you a failure. When you fall, make sure you get up faster than you fell.

Find Some Role Models

When talking about role models, I don't mean the music and movie stars you probably admire for their fashion sense. By "role models," I mean people whose life stories can inspire you to become a better you and reach for greater heights in life. Find people who have been through where and what you are going through, then learn how they overcame their challenges and strategies they adopted to win their life battles.

Whatever It Takes, Make Sure You Leave No Tasks Unaccomplished

One sure thing that helps you build self-discipline is to ensure you complete your current tasks before moving to other tasks. No matter the goal you are working towards — be it losing those unwanted pounds of flesh; starting that new business; learning how to be an expert in music, sports, drawing, or painting; or becoming a better politician — if you are on any of these tasks, you must follow through with the training and learning. It makes you more prepared for becoming the best in what you do.

Chapter 7: Daily Habits That Can Increase Your Level of Self-Discipline

Have an Attitude of Gratitude

Gratitude comes with a whole lot of benefits, from improving the state of your mental health to enhancing your emotional wellbeing. Most importantly, gratitude helps you detach from your state of lack and scarcity. Thinking about the things you desire will make it hard for you to attain the level of self-discipline you need to actually achieve your goals.

Forgive

When it comes to forgiveness, you must learn to forgive both yourself and others to enable you to get ahead in life. Learning to forgive yourself when you err and others when they hurt you is an act of discipline that helps build up your energy for success. Whenever people hurt you, just forgive them and empty your mind of a load of hate and malice. Forgiving people who hurt you helps you release all negative energy that makes you lose your self-discipline. You must get rid of that negative energy, because holding it will make you feel tired, discouraged, and angry all the time. Plus, it subtracts from your capability of thinking.

Meditate

Engaging in meditations helps put your mind at ease. It creates a type of spiritual atmosphere around you to help you grow and become a better you. Meditation sets the stage for you to attain a higher state of self-discipline by clearing the palette of your mind and putting you in the right mood to face the challenges of the day.

Set Active Goals for Each Day

Active goals are active because they can be seen. You make your goals active by putting them down on paper and placing them where they can be seen. Active goals help you build and increase your level of self-discipline, because they give your life daily direction. This is when I talk about daily activities. There's no need to have an extreme objective or dream to set active goals; in fact, there are activities, such as washing the clothes, reading books, cooking, sleeping 8 hours a day, etc., that you will need to do every day. You can start with those home activities to increase your self-discipline.

Eat Right

When you eat the right foods, you help your body store more energy. When your diet is mostly composed of fats, carbohydrates, and proteins, your body dissipates lots of energy processing such foods. When you eat more fruits and veggies, which require less energy to be processed, you will experience an energy boost that will help you pursue your goals with an adequate level of self-discipline. Also, eating at the same time every day will help you to have a healthy life when it comes to ingesting the right nutrients. This way you will avoid having diseases or stomach problems, such as gastritis. Having these health problems will only take part of your time to recover, and you will have to postpone your goals. It is preferable to prevent than to cure.

Get Enough Sleep

There is a direct link between sleep and self-discipline. Whether you give your body enough rest by getting adequate sleep or not goes a long way to determine your ability to stay focused on your goal to achieve self-discipline, and your general wellbeing. Make sure you get 6-8 hours of sleep, no matter how busy you are.

Exercise Daily

Incorporating physical exercises into your daily routines helps you get rid of bad habits and adopt positive habits. If you really want to learn to discipline yourself, make certain physical exercises part of your morning routine. Most people give the excuse that they are too busy or have a lot of worries to get involved in physical exercises. Where such people get it wrong is that they forget they can improve their entire lives through physical exercise.

Stay Organized

Don't just wake up and start working on your goals for the day. Make sure you have your goals and daily tasks arranged in an orderly manner. Arranging your goals in an orderly manner helps you stay organized which is a good sign of self-discipline. Being organized goes beyond having a list of things to do, taking into account priorities. It also involves organizing all areas of your life such as your work table, your drawer, your kitchen cabinets, your wardrobe, your garage, your bedroom, and all other such spaces in your life.

Read

The body is not everything and health does not imply only work out the body. You also have to work out your mind and improve your knowledge and intelligence. There's no better way to do this than reading a book. It is considered one of the best habits a person may have and will definitely guide you to accomplishing your goals. Reading opens the mind to new worlds and offers new life perspectives. I always recommend reading books often. You will learn from it, and you will find different ways to perform your daily activities. You can find encouragement in this, improve your reading and writing skills, and feel more confident in any aspect of your life, due to the acquired knowledge.

Chapter 8: The Psychology of Self-Discipline

The Special Forces Selection is designed to test the minds and bodies of potential operators. They realized a long time ago that the mind is their most important tool. This is why you too have to master your own psychology to reach your goals and take your life to the next level.

Self-discipline is generally an act of will, so it is important to understand how the human mind works. This is done in order to convert understanding to a greater sense of self-control. Over millions of years, the human being has evolved an even more complex brain. Psychology, as a human endeavor, has shed some light into the mysteries of the mind, finally allowing us to see how things affect or motivate people and how our environment affects how we react to things that occur.

Self-Image

The way people perceive themselves affects how they react to the world. This is shaped by how they have raised and the people that have surrounded them. The environment they grew up in has shaped how they see themselves. There are people with low self-esteem, and this makes them believe that they are unworthy of good things or that they are incapable of achieving perfection.

On the other hand, there are others who have an inflated sense of self-worth, and they believe that they deserve everything without actually having to do much. These people, though they may seem powerful on the outside, are in fact hollow. Cracks in their tough shell will show overwhelming insecurity that they have spent a lifetime hiding. If a man is on the quest to become a true alpha male, he must be able to know the truth about himself and not give in to insecurity or the temptation to take the easy road by simply hiding under a facade.

Locus of Control

A person on the path to self-improvement must find out whether he blames others for the things that happen to him or if he blames himself for what happens to him. If a person blames others all the time for everything that happens, their locus of control is said to be external, which means that they let go of his power to fate or "destiny." This is the weak man's approach, especially if he believes that he is unable to change anything that happens to him. He is weak-minded and weak-willed, and he thinks that whatever happens to him is because of random chance and other people or events. This is a lazy and weak approach to life.

On the other hand, a man whose locus of control is internal tends to see everything as his fault, and if this goes to the extreme, he ends up being too overwhelmed by what is happening to him and even to the world. He might blame himself about something that happened to someone totally unrelated to him. This is unrealistic. We go back to the topic of the self-image: the man must be able to have the right information about himself in order to act upon it.

Classical Conditioning

To challenge the idea that psychology was an armchair pseudoscience, the behaviorist movement, which included the psychologist Ivan Pavlov, brought the scientific method into the field through experimentation. Pavlov was able to show the process of training and conditioning by measuring how much dogs salivated every time a bell was rung to signify food. After the experimenter rings the bell, they put the food out. Soon, even when the experimenter does not bring out food, the mere ringing of the bell makes the dogs react as if they are ready for food. This is called conditioning, and another way to apply this concept is reward and punishment.

People and animals tend to stay from punishment, and they tend to look for rewards. So, rewards will make us keep doing what we were doing in order to get the pleasure of that reward. Punishments work the other way around, so the balance of both reward and punishment will effectively condition a person to a certain kind of action. Because we were born with the capacity to rule ourselves, we can consciously apply this method to ourselves in order to achieve the kind of action we want to learn. Ask yourself how much pain you will get if you don't take action. For example, how much pain will you experience if you don't study for your exam? Maybe you won't graduate. Now think about the short-term pain of studying versus the long-term pain of not graduating. Now think of the reward or pleasure you will get if you do study. You will graduate with a degree and be respected by others. So in this way, you can trick yourself into doing things that you don't feel like doing.

Psychology of Motivation

When people are asked who will win between a lion and a man in an arena, most people answer the lion because it is more powerful, and it has evolved to be stronger than the man. Unless that man is the mythical Hercules, the lion will no doubt devour him. However, this does not take into consideration the sort of evolution that humanity has gone through in the past millions of years. The human has evolved a more complex brain and the ability to innovate and create weapons. Thus, a fairer fight would be between a lion and a man armed with weapons.

Humans are more complex than animals, and the

difference is evident in our desire to become greater than ourselves. This book is already a testament to that. Thus, in motivating a man to become better than himself, it is important that he knows what he is fighting for. He needs a goal, and a way to know whether or not he has achieved it. Not knowing what he is fighting for, even the hardened warrior will fail. A man with a purpose is unstoppable.

Once a person has decided on their goal, they must begin to act. Success is being and doing what you want now, and that can only be achieved if you act immediately and act as if that success is already present now. Soon, even without thinking about it, the goal will have already been reached. It is also important, then, to trust in the process or habit through the continuous application of self-discipline.

Chapter 9: Immerse Yourself in the Culture of Self-Discipline

Surround Yourself with Disciplined People

When developing your own self-discipline, you need to surround yourself with people who have the same goals and aspirations as you. It is even better if you can find people who are very dedicated to their work. By surrounding yourself with these types of people, you will have someone with which you can compare yourself. If you are competitive by nature, having people around you who are good at what they do can ignite your competitive spirit. This can be a great source of extrinsic motivation.

Examine Your Internal Beliefs

Your internal beliefs, ideas, and attitude set the tone for your success and life in general. The saddest part about these beliefs is that they are so deeply ingrained in our subconscious mind that we are often unaware of them. These ideas may be sown in our mind since a very young change through childhood experiences or tough situations within our family or immediate environment. For instance, if your caregivers pressurized you with high expectations and made you feel small if you were unable to meet them, you may have grown up with the belief that you are good for nothing.

Build an Attitude of Gratitude

One of the strategies to attract even more in your life is to be thankful for what you already have. This is one of the best ways to condition your subconscious for success. Counting your blessings allows you to curb more negative, self-defeating, and hopeless thoughts and beliefs, and discipline your thinking for success. It is time to turn your negative thinking upside down and be grateful for all the gifts you have been blessed with. It will change the frequency of your thoughts from negative and self-limiting to more positive, constructive and hopeful.

Build a Mindset of Converting Challenges into Opportunities

Contrary to popularly held beliefs, winners are not folks who have never experienced setbacks or failures. In fact, they are individuals who turn these challenges upside down into learning opportunities.

Decide to Transform

If you are unhappy with your life, money, or professional life, start by changing your habits, actions, mindset, thoughts, behavior, attitude, and so on now. All you require to be rich and successful is within you. It is inside you, waiting to be tapped. You just have to dip into it to experience roaring huge success. At times, we wonder why talented and passionate people are unable to achieve improvement and success, while other people who may not be as skilled witness greater success and glory. It is merely a matter of mindset that drives people to work hard and chase their dreams despite challenges. Perseverance is often the clinching factor between success and failure.

Developing Your Own Group of Highly Disciplined People

Find self-improvement buddies

You need a buddy who will keep an eye on you and make sure that you do the tasks properly and on time. Ideally, you need to find a buddy who also wants to develop his own self-discipline. If you have a friend undergoing the same difficulties as you, you will have a better chance of convincing yourself to be committed to the tasks required by this book.

Set punishments for failure or unfinished tasks

In the military, people complete the tasks that they need to do because they do not have a choice. The drill sergeants remove the idea of having a choice. Either you do what they want, or you quit the military life because you are too weak. This prepares the soldiers for active service. When they are in the field, they are accustomed to following orders, and they do not question the decisions of their superiors. In this kind of practice, you are able to learn the value of trusting your superiors. If you are capable of following your superiors, you will be able to set your own rules soon and follow them by yourself.

Just like in the military, the punishment that you set should be physical in nature. Push-ups and squats are the common punishments among the basic training of all the branches of the military. You could also think of undesirable chores like cleaning the backyard or the toilet and doing your buddy's laundry.

Now that you have the necessary requirements for developing Special Forces culture, you need to learn the habits that you need to integrate into your life. These habits are designed to make you disciplined from your waking to your sleeping hour.

Chapter 10: The Power of Self-Discipline

Self-discipline is exactly what it says: the ability to discipline oneself. It is the ability to know what to do in situations and the fortitude to actually do what is correct in each situation. It is a habit that is vital to daily success. Truly successful people are usually highly disciplined people.

No one is born with the ability to truly self-discipline. Babies only care about being taken care of and having their needs met. As children grow, their parents are in charge of their discipline, or at least in the beginning. Parents make the rules, and children follow them because small children lack the thought processes needed to make good decisions on a regular basis. Small children only see the here-and-now, the immediate gratification.

They do not know and do not care that a bigger, better reward might be in store for them if they wait patiently. They lack foresight. As children grow up, they begin to see the reasoning behind their parents' rules. They begin to make choices that mirror the choices their parents have made for them in the past. They show that they are learning to discipline themselves. At this point, the parents may begin to step back a little and loosen the reins. They may allow the child a bit more freedom in making decisions, with the understanding that the parent is available if the choice turns out to be unfavorable. In this way, the child learns in the safety of the home and with the protection of the parents to make good choices and formulate good decisions. The child learns to self-discipline.

In a perfect world, this is the way children would be raised. Unfortunately, this is the real world and not a perfect one. The problem is not that parents do not care about their children; it is that many parents do not know how to teach the art of self-discipline to their children. Maybe the parents are not self-disciplined, maybe the parents feel the child will learn it eventually, or maybe the parents simply do not want to let go of their complete control over the child. For whatever reason, most children are not taught self-discipline as a way of life and reach adulthood with no clue of how to be in charge of themselves.

However, the good news is that self-discipline can be learned. While best learned while growing up, as a part of learning to be an adult, it is possible to learn as an adult and begin to practice self-discipline skills immediately. Moreover, by learning self-discipline in adulthood, the person has a total buy-in to the idea. This is a personal choice. This is something that needs to be done in order to enjoy a better life. This does not mean that learning self-discipline as an adult will be easier or faster, but at least, the adult who makes the conscious choice to become more self-disciplined has a personal stake in its success.

Self-discipline is nothing more than managing one's own personal affairs. It is a way of behaving where people automatically choose to do what should be done, as opposed to what would more preferably be done. It is studying for a test instead of going to a party. It is washing dirty laundry on a regular basis, so that clean clothes are always available. It is following a budget so that future financial goals can be realized. Self-discipline is that inner voice controlling outward actions. It is using willpower to become mentally tough enough to control one's actions by oneself.

Almost anything that a person does to focus on an end goal rather than immediate satisfaction is a form of practicing self-discipline. The underlying problem is that it is always much easier to follow the path of impulse. Impulse is fun. Impulse is now. Impulse allows for joining the group and having a fun night on the town instead of studying and doing laundry. Impulse is the exact opposite of self-discipline.

Practicing self-discipline requires great self-knowledge. Think about that for a minute. Keep the plan simple. Self-discipline does not need to be complicated. The idea of self-discipline itself is actually a very simple concept. A plan for achieving self-discipline should be as simple as possible while encompassing all aspects needed to reach the goal. A complicated plan may be impossible to achieve and will probably lead to defeat, and giving up is not an option on the road to self-discipline.

Self-discipline allows for more time to do the things that will bring satisfaction and less of the things that provide no growth or satisfaction. Self-disciplined people set a goal and work toward it.

Self-discipline takes an extreme amount of energy to achieve. It is not just choosing to be self-disciplined; it must be constantly worked at, and that takes energy. This will require good lifestyle practices. Eat healthily, sleep regularly, exercise when possible — all these activities will energize the body and mind and make working toward the goal of self-discipline more easily attainable.

Chapter 11: Building Mental Toughness

You need to be mentally tough to squash and stomp out any doubts that may creep into your mind. Mental toughness is a valuable asset when it comes to overcoming your distractions and becoming a more self-disciplined person. Mentally tough people are not quitters. They have the drive to do what it takes to succeed; to get back up ten times after falling for nine.

A strong character is also essential for self-discipline. Often, a lack of self-discipline is a sign of weak character. Building a character will enable you to withstand any challenge you may face. If you are successful, self-discipline will never be a struggle in your life.

Why Do You Need Mental Toughness?

Mental toughness is required for managing emotions.

It is unavoidable that people will experience emotions. Emotions are a naturally occurring state of mind that results from a person's surroundings, moods, and relationships and interactions with other people. Because emotions are naturally occurring, they may actually overtake a person's thoughts and become their main focus if a person lets them do so. This is where mental toughness comes in. Mental toughness gives a person the ability to control, to some extent, their emotions, as well as the way in which they react to them and how much these emotions take over the person's mind.

Mental toughness is required for controlling and handling your thoughts.

Thoughts differ from emotions due to the fact that they are not always about feelings. In fact, a significant portion of our time is spent thinking about things that do not have much to do with our emotions. You may think about whether or not you are going to be able to finish your homework or work project on time. Although the thought of not finishing the assignment on time may evoke some feelings and emotions, the thought of whether or not you will finish the assignment on time is not primarily based on emotion.

Mental toughness is the key to willpower.

Most people would be surprised to find out that willpower or a lack thereof is the primary obstacle that most people face when trying to better themselves. You would probably assume that it would be money, race, or class; however, in this day and age, these hurdles have been lessened by the slow growth of acceptance in the workplace.

Mental toughness is required to navigate through trying times.

During times when you are doing well, have some money in the bank, your relationships are good, you are in good health, and you are rather happy, your mental toughness may not be called in as much unless it is in certain high-pressure situations. However, if you ever experience hard times, such as the death of a spouse or a child, loss of a job and source of income, a natural disaster or something of that nature, then it is very important for you to have mental toughness to get through the situation the best that you can and get back on your feet. Hard times really are a test of your will. And hard times can happen to anybody, whether they expect it and have planned for it or not.

To establish a winner's mind

Working on and establishing mental toughness is like setting a standard of excellence for yourself that causes you to strive for a higher level of excellence that you may have ordinarily strived for you had you not worked to cultivate your mind. It is like setting a higher level of expectations for yourself, and you are aware of what these expectations are. Oftentimes, thinking that you can do or excel at something is half the battle and when trying to establish mental toughness, conditioning your mind for winning thoughts processes is very important. Your mindset can help you with your willpower, dedication, time management, and the other essential things that you need to do to establish your goals and to succeed at the things that you set out to do.

Mental toughness promotes longevity in your career or goals

Mental toughness is what allows you to stick around in your career or at your set goals. For instance, let's say that you want to be a dancer. You must undergo a great deal of practice and training to get started. Then you go on a number of auditions, several of which will be rejections. You may hear criticism of your skills in a not-so-friendly manner, maybe even a little hurtful. If you ever want to get on Broadway, you have to go through all of this and that just to make it in the show. After that, there are rehearsals, shows, and more rehearsals and shows. If you do not have a strong mind, you are not going to make it that long under these conditions and deadlines. It is very important that you use your mental strength to keep pushing on and to help you understand what you are working for.

Mental toughness allows you to handle distractions and keep your focus

Building mental toughness allows you to keep your focus and not be swayed by distractions when they come your way. This is very important, because life is full of distractions, and you will run into a large number of them if you want to achieve lofty goals. These distractions will not knock you off your game as much if you have a strong mind and the ability to focus.

Mental toughness is the answer to being distracted. Although mental toughness does not allow you to block out emotions and emotional situations, it does allow you to handle your emotions and emotional situations in the proper manner so that you can address these issues at the proper time and still be able to function during the day.

Mental toughness teaches you to prioritize

In life, there will be a great number of things that you need to get done that may cause you to neglect your priorities. This is simply a fact of life that cannot be changed, and you need to have the mental toughness to figure out what your priorities are and how to get everything else done without neglecting them.

Mental toughness teaches patience

You cannot have everything at once, and mental toughness will help you with patience in the same way that it helps with willpower. You cannot expect immediate results. Time and patience are part of the key to success in the long run. You can expect to get everything at one time; therefore, patience is a virtue that mental toughness instills in us.

Mental toughness gives you greater life satisfaction

Mental toughness helps to increase a person's life satisfaction. This is because it gives you the basic tools you need to succeed and the drive to do it. Mental strong people are able to handle life, in general, better than people who lack mental strength. They can control their emotions, work more efficiently, they are better listeners, and they bond better with others.

Mental toughness allows you to reduce stress and anxiety

Stress and anxiety, a subject that will be discussed in more detail later in this book, are harmful to your mind and body if left unchecked and allowed to fester. Stress causes a number of health problems, both mental and physical. It can affect everything in your life as well. You may become agitated when you get stressed out and take it out on those around you including family members, children, coworkers, friends, strangers, and more. This can cause problems in relationships that may be hard to fix if done repeatedly, over a period of time, or if the stressful situation is not fixed.

How to Build Mental Toughness:

Develop a strong support system

Create a positive, strong, and encouraging support system to gain strength from whenever required. During challenging times, we must be able to share our feelings with a close, trustworthy, and motivating group of people. Exchange thoughts and feelings, enlist the support of people you trust, learn about people's journey, gain constructive feedback, enlist support, and discuss possible alternatives. The people you surround yourself with contribute largely to your thoughts and mental framework. Speaking to trusted people can help you gain new insights, views, and solutions about challenging situations, which in turn boosts your mental toughness.

Take cold showers

You might think this is unnecessary suffering, but it is not because taking cold showers has a lot of benefits such as boosting your immune system, increasing levels of testosterone, reducing inflammation, and so on. When the cold water touches your skin for the first time, try not to yell or wince. Just bear it and keep your mind and body as relaxed as possible by taking deep breaths. Try to stay in the cold water for at least 30 seconds and just make it longer as you get used to the coldness.

Minimize social media usage

It takes a lot of mental toughness to unplug from social media. You can either stop using it completely or try to use it only when necessary, like for communication or sharing important stuff. But minimize social media usage as much as you can and just spend your free time doing more productive things. Believe it or not, Steve Jobs didn't let his kids use iPads because he knows how toxic it can get once people start to go online and use social media.

Get out of bed right away

When you hear your alarm go off in the morning, do not press the snooze button, and do not stay in your bed even for just one minute longer. Get out of bed right away and do something to keep your blood flowing. Splash your face with cold water, make coffee or tea, prepare breakfast, and just do anything to wake yourself up. This is all just mind over matter. And you will feel a lot better later on when you realize how much you were able to finish in a day because you woke up early.

Sleep on the floor

You can also try sleeping on the floor once in a while. You don't necessarily need to give up your comfortable bed for good. Just do this from time to time to help you build your mental toughness. For a really tough challenge, sleep without a blanket. Use a thin sheet if you are not ready for the difficulty level.

Do small exercises

This will not be your regular full-blown workout. That is

another thing that you should be doing even if you are not trying to lose weight because it will keep your body strong and healthy. These mini workouts are workouts that you can incorporate in your everyday life.

Move slowly

You might think that this tip is counterintuitive, because slowness is often not associated with success and achieving goals. But this does not literally mean working at a slower pace. It just means that you do not make impulsive actions and snap decisions.

Get dirty

Some people are so afraid to get themselves dirty because getting dirty is way out of their comfort zone. Although being clean is something that we should all strive for, there is nothing wrong with getting yourself dirty from time to time.

Read

Reading a book can make you tougher mentally because it helps you improve your mental focus for a long period of time. Read a book for a couple of hours every day; that can teach you a thing or two about delayed gratification, unlike television and online videos that are passive entertainment and do not really contribute anything to improving your mental toughness. Reading is also an activity that allows you to use your mind actively and learning new words and information is always a welcome bonus.

Take a break

When something doesn't help you achieve the desired results, go on a break or change your strategy rather than giving up. Tackle the task with a rejuvenated, fresher, and brand-new perspective after recharging your batteries. True success and glory come to people who do not quit.

Build a mindset

When faced with tough situations, brainstorm. Think of

solutions, ideas, alternatives, and possibilities for resolving the situation instead of giving up. There are various ways to work out a solution strategy by keeping your mind more open, flexible, and fearless. You may require a change in the approach or a slight strategy change. Recognize various ways to deal with a challenging or overwhelming situation.

Develop a sense of humor

This is a simple, easy, and enjoyable hack for people to develop mental toughness, yet a good number of people fail to see its virtues. When you experience challenges, humor can help you sail through the situation with ease. Look at the lighter side of things. This helps us overcome stress, disappointment, and anxiety connected to it. You gain a totally different perspective about challenges by viewing them using the lens of humor.

Build a positive or constructive view of your skills and abilities

An individual's sense of self-esteem, self-confidence, and self-image is largely affected by perseverance. Keep reminding yourself about your strengths, achievements, skills, abilities, and wonderful moments. Make a list of tough situations you have tackled, and how you battled them. Draw inspiration from winning and positive moments of the past.

Observe your self-talk

What is your mental talk sound like? If it isn't positive, abundant, and successful, latch on to a different frequency. Our self-talk has the power to determine our chances of success. This self-talk can help us sail through challenging circumstances or dive into failure. Realign your self-talk for success by making it more positive, balanced, and constructive.

How Mental Strength Improves Self-Discipline

Mental strength is one of the most important elements of self-discipline. Knowing how it contributes to self-discipline will help you to see why you need to be constantly working to enhance it.

When you are mentally strong, it allows you to conquer self-doubt so that it is not able to interfere with your level of discipline or cause you to procrastinate out of fear.

Motivation comes from your mental strength. When you are not mentally strong, you will find that it is much easier to lose your motivation before you even have a chance to take full advantage of it.

You can easily tune out comments and advice that are simply not going to help you. This is critical for self-discipline, since it is all about efficiency and removing unnecessary baggage.

When you are mentally strong, you are able to face your fears. Fears are one of the biggest reasons that people are not able to develop a strong sense of self-discipline.

You can more easily rebound from failure with mental strength. When you quickly come back from failure, it's more difficult to disrupt your ability to be disciplined.

Lastly, you can easily learn from your mistakes. Remember that learning and accountability are paramount when working to enhance your discipline level.

Chapter 12: The Truth about Motivation

Only when you invest the necessary energy into your self-discipline will it function correctly, taking you to your desired destination.

Creating Your Motivation

One of the most important energies that your self-discipline relies on is motivation. This is probably the single thing that keeps so many people from achieving the success that they so desperately desire. No amount of self-discipline can help you to achieve your goals in life unless you have the motivation needed to keep things moving along. In short, self-discipline without motivation is no different than an engine without gas.

Therefore, the first thing you need to do is to ensure that your goals actually belong to you and that they aren't ideas placed into your mind by someone else. Before you begin to plan and plot your way to a destination you need to decide that the destination is where you really want to go. If it isn't, you will face an uphill battle each and every step along the way. Time after time, you will struggle with the obstacles and pitfalls along the way to achieving your goal, without any real incentive to persevere.

Regardless of whether you are pursuing a dream to please your parents, a spouse, or even social norms, it all boils down to the same scenario. If the dream doesn't come from your heart, you won't have the fire in your belly that drives you to your success.

Once you have determined that your goal truly belongs to you, the next step is to discover the reason behind the goal. Every goal has an underlying cause, something that makes a particular goal worth pursuing.

Alternatively, you might want to achieve a goal because of the lifestyle you believe it will offer you. No matter what your motivation is, the important thing is to discover it so that it can help fuel the self-discipline you need in order to achieve your dream.

Reward and Punishment

Another way to establish motivation in your life is to create a system of reward and punishment. This might seem a bit harsh at first, especially the punishment part; however, it's not as bad as it sounds. The idea of punishment for failure shouldn't be interpreted as causing yourself pain and suffering whenever you fall short; rather, it is a matter of withholding certain pleasures from yourself when you engage in negative behavior. By withholding things that bring pleasure when you engage in negative behavior and indulging in them when you put forth your best efforts, you will create a very real value system in your mind that will redefine how you see self-discipline.

One of the reasons why so many people never pursue a dream or a meaningful goal is that they have an easy enough life without achieving their dreams. People can indulge in their favorite coffee drinks, fancy pastries, or any other number of tasty temptations any time, any day. This turns those things that would be rewards into everyday items, removing their true value as well as the potential they have for helping you to succeed. By withholding such things from yourself when you go astray, you create a sense of punishment that you will want to avoid. Again, this isn't about creating pain in your life; rather, it is about encouraging you to steer clear of certain behaviors or activities.

Creating a Competitive Environment

Finally, there is the aspect of creating a competitive environment. What most people don't realize is that the energy in their mind is directly affected by the energy of their surroundings. Thus, the more time a person spends in a negative environment, the more negative their energies will become. The very same thing holds true in terms of people. When a person surrounds themselves with negative people, their mindset will become negative as a result. The solution is to create a competitive environment. This is what is meant by placing yourself in the right places and around the right people in order to bring out your best in terms of effort, talent, and overall self-discipline.

The first step to creating a competitive environment is to distinguish the difference between positive and negative environments clearly. Any place that encourages laziness, self-pity, negative thinking and other such toxic energies is a place that you need to avoid. The last thing you need to do is to put yourself in an environment that will encourage the behaviors you are trying to rid yourself of. Such environments can include cheap bars where people go to drown their sorrows in alcohol and thus avoid facing their problems head-on. Basically, any place that attracts deadbeats, dropouts, and those with low self-esteem are places you want to steer well clear of.

In addition to avoiding negative places and people, it is critical that you find positive places and people to replace them with. Just as the negative energy from spiteful, lazy people can influence your own energy, so too can the positive energy from successful, highly motivated people.

Chapter 13: Persistence Is the Key to Self-Discipline

The desire for a more self-disciplined personality will not be enough unless you persist and are willing to keep that momentum going. Persistence is another important trait you'll need to build a strong character. Your very success will depend on your ability to persist even when the odds are not in your favor. Setbacks will happen, wrenches will be thrown in your plan. You must persist in the face of them all. That is the epitome of what self-discipline is all about.

Persistence is something you absolutely need when it comes to adopting greater self-discipline. You have heard the word, and you surely know what it means by definition. However, what is important is that you understand its importance, its role for greater self-discipline, and what persistence feels like to you. This will make it much easier to ensure that you are staying on track and constantly working to ensure that you exercise persistence in all areas of your life.

Being persistent means that no matter the opposition or difficulty that you face, you remain in the course of action that you have created for yourself. This is one of the cornerstones of self-discipline. It is important that you are constantly able to keep pushing forward no matter the adversity that you face.

When you are working on replacing your bad habits with good habits, you have to be persistent. This will help to prevent you from giving up when it starts to get tough.

How to Improve Your Persistence

You know what persistence can do and what it means for improving your success, but how exactly do you work to improve your level of persistence? There are multiple things that you can do, and none are that difficult. The key is that you have to identify how persistent you are now so that you understand how much work you have to do to get to the level of persistence you need to ensure an optimal level of self-discipline.

Try the following common methods on improving your level of persistence:

- Know what you desire and want, and make a visual of it so that you have a picture in mind of what you are working so hard for.
- Know what causes you to become motivated, since motivation can spur you to get started with pursuing a goal.
- Once you have a goal, you need to outline the steps that you have to take to ensure that you are able to stay on track in accomplishing your goal.
- It is important to make sure that your mental attitude is positive, and that negativity is tackled as soon as it starts.
- Find people who can help you build your persistence and keep them close.

Persistence can be a surprisingly rewarding quality. When you power through a task (along with willpower), the result is going to make you feel much happier and better about yourself. As part of this ripple effect, those feelings will drive you to want to do more, to see just how far you can go if you only persist on a task. Even if you were to have bucket loads of self-discipline, if you do not persist, the success that may be within your grasp may end up sliding further out of reach.

Why is Persistence Such an Important Quality as You Become a More Self-Disciplined Person?

- Persistence is among the first signs that you are transforming into a more ambitious person. Setting all the goals and actions plans in the world is not going to be enough if you are going to give up and not persevere each time you are knocked on your bottom. If you want to become a successful person, ambition and drive are going to be the levers which are going to help drive you to the top.
- It makes victories that much more valuable. If success always came easy, we would never learn to appreciate it. Being a persistent person will allow let you appreciate every accomplish and make every victory taste just a little bit sweeter because you know you poured your heart, soul, blood, sweat, and tears into making it happen.
- It is good for character building because persistence is living proof that you have it within you to achieve a goal. Each time you push through a difficult period, you will emerge that much stronger and better.
- It will fine-tune you regarding your weaknesses and fears. Part of achieving success is to be able to identify them. When you persist through one weakness and overcome it, you will automatically start looking for the next weakness that you can work through.

Persistence as a Part of Your Character

Being ready for success in life will partly be dependent on your response to setbacks. Setbacks have a way of frustrating our emotions with feelings of despondency and discouragement. We end up confused as to why it has happened in spite of all the effort you've put in. These seemingly small failures may even push us to give in.

Setbacks give you the perfect opportunity to rise to the challenge, to pull in persistence and self-discipline together.

You'll remember that what matters is not how hard or how many times you fall. It's your ability to get back up and dust yourself off that really counts. Shake off the frustration. Build yourself and believe that you can overcome this trial. Keep the following key points in mind:

Be Optimistic

Having an optimistic outlook is the first and most important key to developing persistence. It's the unwavering belief that no matter what happens; things will work out in the end. You can develop optimism by building and also improving your self-belief and self-confidence. Persistent and disciplined people do not just sit idly, feeling sorry for themselves whenever challenges arise.

Look to your role models and your mentors. They would not be where they are today if they had allowed setbacks and difficulties to stop them and the challenges have surely been many. Yet, they remain optimistic.

No Room for Excuses

Pointing fingers and blaming the hand you've been dealt with is not a winning attitude. Unaccountability will only feed into that negativity cycle of feeling sorry for yourself. The result is often diminished willpower and, eventually, giving in to a seemingly difficult task.

Focus on the Solution

The key to winning at persistence is to focus on the solution, not the problem. You have to realize that setbacks, however difficult, are ultimately temporary. Thus, always have the solution as a priority.

Every time you face an unexpected setback, train your mind in such a way that its first impulse is to think and focus on resolving the current issue. Staying focused on a solution will give you the determination to persist and keep going until the setback is resolved. Use self-discipline as a springboard for that persistence so that nothing deters you.

Identify Problem Areas

It's important that you find the areas in your life where persistence will be most helpful. These areas will most likely be where fear is holding you back. Identify specific areas and write them down so you can better reflect on them. Ask yourself why persistence has lacked in this area before. What can you do differently this time? Create an action plan that is detailed and precise.

Think of Setbacks as Gifts

Considering a setback as a gift instead of a curse may be the last thing on your mind. However, this method actually works. If you think about the past challenges and setbacks that you faced that you managed to overcome eventually anyway, instead of looking at the downside, consider the takeaway lessons each setback left you with. Did it make you a much stronger person? Did it turn out to be a blessing in disguise? Did it add something of value to your life in a way you might not otherwise have had the opportunity of experiencing? If you can train yourself to view each setback as a gift instead of a demotivating element, you will do wonders to transform your persistence and levels of self-discipline.

Chapter 14: Habits and their Role in Self-Discipline

Cultivating good habits is a very effective way of becoming self-disciplined. This is because most of what we do and how we behave daily are determined by our habits. Therefore, having the right habits will go a long way in bringing discipline into our lives.

We tend to have some bad habits that have a negative effect on our lives because over a long time the neural pathways become a part of us, and it becomes very hard to shake off the bad habits and develop good ones. But if you can make a conscious decision to develop good habits in your life, you'll find that becoming disciplined will be easier. It is not an overnight process, and it takes time to form new habits.

Get Started Even When You Do Not Feel Like It

Successful people become who they are because through sheer willpower and determination, they rose above their weaknesses and developed good qualities and habits. You must be ready to have a greater mastery of your personality and exhibit the strength to overcome all obstacles, including yourself, until you succeed. Ability to do the right things even when you don't feel like it is the means to self-confidence and achieving greatness.

Force Yourself until It Becomes Routine

If you are feeling reluctant to start working on something important, convince yourself that you will do it for only 5 minutes. It could be performing aerobic exercises, replying to emails, or meditating for a short period. Once you start, you will discover that the activity will continue for more than the 5 minutes than your mind is conditioned to do; this is because you have overcome the initial barrier of personal resistance and will get into a state of flow.

Set Reminders

Maintaining focus can be hard; therefore, to remain on task, ensure that your goals are not far away from your mind and attention. Remind yourself about your goals regularly by using journals, diaries, and reminders to stay on top of your daily activities.

Continuous Personal Improvement

To become the best you can be you must consistently improve your knowledge. Dedicate effort to investing in yourself by expanding your knowledge and skills.

A way of doing this is to read daily, up to an hour if you can. Having knowledge about your goals can be very helpful, such as reading relevant articles and newsletters, you can easily learn about a variety of diets to live by if your goal is to eat healthily and stay fit.

Habits and How They Impact Self-Control

Habits have the capacity to impact our self-control by either supporting our ability to have self-control or by taking away from our ability to have self-control. Our habits are essentially regular tendencies or behaviors that we repeat on a regular basis, and often, they are hard to change or get over. Habits exist on what psychologists call habit loops, which look like this: first, you are triggered to initiate a certain behavior, then you engage in that behavior, then you achieve your desired outcome, and then you are rewarded for feeling as if you have accomplished something.

The Importance of Identifying Bad Habits

If you want to develop your self-discipline, it is crucial that you begin learning how to discover your bad habits. Knowing how to identify and understand your bad habits is the key to being able to actually transcend these habits so that you can begin truly engaging in self-discipline. A person who has mastered self-discipline is able to easily identify when they are engaging in bad habits, how these bad habits are impacting them, and what they can do to minimize or eliminate these bad habits in their life. Many times, a self-disciplined person will find that the more they recognize and shift their bad habits, the more they can do this with ease.

They become so used to understanding how their mind works and what their attachments to their habits look like that a person who has mastered self-discipline can begin shifting and transcending limiting habits and behaviors rapidly and with ease. They become aware of the fact that a bad habit is not a part of their identity but rather a habitual behavior that they are participating in, and so, they can begin participating in new habits with ease. They do not identify themselves with any of the actions that they take, even repeated actions, so they have an easier time releasing them.

Positive Habits and Self-Discipline

Ensuring that you are productive and self-disciplined depends largely on the habits that you are working to develop. There are certain positive habits that will play into this more than others. These are the ones that you want to start working on now, and they include:

- Make sure that your workspace is clean and organized so that you have no excuse to procrastinate.
- Take 90 minutes every day to focus on the tasks that are most important.
- Start working smarter, so that you can focus for fewer hours, but still be more productive than you were.
- Turn off your cellphone and disengage from social media so that it is not distracting you.
- Check your email no more than once every two hours and make sure to keep each email session to no more than 10 minutes each time.
- Delegate when you can, so that you can lessen your load and get more done in less time.
- Determine everything that distracts you and promptly get rid of it without making any excuses.
- Spend 10 minutes each morning roughly planning out your day and highlighting which tasks need to take precedence over the others.
- Make sure to take your lunch break away from your desk. This helps to give your mind a little time to unwind and replenish so that you have the mental energy needed to complete your day.
- List what you need to get done every day in order of importance, and always work from the top to the bottom of the list so that the most tedious tasks are done first and out of the way.
- Admit your mistakes and create a plan to banish the habits that are hindering your productivity.
- If there are issues blocking your productivity that are related to others, talk to these people about it and work together to solve the issues.
- Spend 10 minutes being active when you are feeling tired to boost your energy levels.

Creating Good Habits to Eliminate Bad Habits

If you find that your productivity is really being destroyed by your own bad habits, it may be time for you to begin developing positive habits that are going to replace these bad habits. Learning how to replace your productivity-busting habits with new habits that are going to help you boost your productivity and increase your self-discipline overall can help you begin to develop a deeper sense of self-discipline.

This way, you are also able to become more productive and achieve more overall. In the end, your habits can begin to serve you rather than prevent you from achieving your desires, which leads to a greater capacity to create all that you desire.

How to Develop New Habits Effectively

Once you have learned how to identify your bad habits, the next step is learning how to develop new habits! New habits can be developed as a way to replace old bad habits, or they can be developed organically to give you new, effective strategies in an area where a habit may be more effective than having to consciously think everything through.

The truth is, there are many ways that you can develop new habits in your life. The best way to do it effectively, however, is to understand how your brain naturally develops habit loops and then use that process to your advantage so that you can stimulate the development of habits on purpose. By purposefully engaging in the behaviors that trigger habit loops and lock in habits, you can ensure that you are developing your habits on purpose and that they are serving you, rather than holding you back.

The best way, then, to develop habits on purpose is to identify a trigger, choose a response, and then respond to that trigger and celebrate the fulfillment of what you want or need. A big key here is stimulating an emotional response, as emotions are how your brain and body know that something is desirable or undesirable. In other words, if the response to your fulfillment of a certain action is positive, such as happiness, relief, or comfort, your brain is going to see that as being positive, and it is going to want to engage in that behavior again. If, however, your response to the fulfillment is neutral or negative, your brain is going to see it as either pointless or unwanted, and therefore, it is going to avoid engaging in the behavior again. At the end of the day, your brain is obsessed with positive emotions because these serve as a form of feedback that tells your brain that what it is doing is keeping you on the right track.

If you are replacing a habit, what you engage in to develop your new habit is going to be slightly different. Pay attention and use the steps that are relevant to what you want to achieve to ensure that you are getting the outcome you desire.

Improving Your Good Habits

Once you adopt a good habit, you have to make it stick. There are several methods that you can start using now to ensure that your newly-gained good habits are ones that are going to be a part of your life for the long-term. In order to improve your good habits:

- Commit yourself to use the good habit for just 30 days, to start with.
- Make sure that you give your new good habit some attention on a daily basis.
- Approximately 14 days into your new habit, remind yourself about your goals and check to ensure that you are on track.
- Keep it simple, and only focus on improving a single good habit at a time.
- Create a trigger that will remind you to give attention to your new habit.
- Ensure that you are consistent in how you choose to go about improving your good habit.
- Find a person that will help you to stay accountable to yourself so that if you slip up, you can immediately get back on track.
- If the bad habit you replaced the good with makes you feel like you have lost something by this point, find something positive to replace it with.

- Get rid of temptations that are threatening to throw you off track.
- Do not be afraid to be imperfect. In fact, embrace imperfection.
- Think of this process as an experiment, because when it seems less permanent, you will find that it is easier to work with.

Chapter 15: Self-Discipline Strategies

Developing a Growth Mindset

A growth mindset is essentially a name for someone who is open-minded and willing to learn and search for solutions to that which they are going through in life. If you have a growth mentality, you are focused on developing your skills and finding ways to move through obstacles that may present themselves along your journey so that you can continue to develop along your path. This way, regardless of what you are up against in life, you are willing to find a way to grow through it and advance toward your goals.

Developing a growth mindset requires you to begin learning how to intentionally open your mind so that you can keep finding your way to your next stage of growth. There are many strategies that you can use that help you develop your growth mindset, but I am going to share the best ones with you, starting with learning to shift how you view challenges in your life.

Define Your Goals

Define a goal; this goal is like fuel in the tank of your car. Defining a goal gives you direction: what do want to accomplish? Why do you want it? Break down the goal into small parts, because this gives you the ability to see a path from where you are to where you want to be. Make a plan that you can follow to bring you closer to your end of year goal. Now it's easy to get carried away with this. You're not going to be good at first, relax and make a simple plan you can execute immediately.

Don't Cheat!

To become disciplined, you must pick a goal and stick to it. Sticking to the plan is what will make you disciplined. In sticking to your daily plan, you will have to put it before anything or anyone else. I find that if you can tackle your plan in the morning, you are pretty much guaranteed to succeed for that day.

Develop the Skill of Self-Motivation

Many people find that they are much more motivated to change when they have a friend who is dealing with the same issues. And that's the problem: most of your friends are just like you in that regard, and they can't really help. Don't misunderstand me — your friends can help and encourage you, but if you depend on other people's energy to keep you on track, then eventually you're going to go off track. It's that simple.

Take Care of Yourself

It's of the utmost importance not to lose momentum once you get it going, you must schedule breaks. After your most important task is finished on time for the week, schedule a nice dinner; or whatever makes you happiest as your treat. Now the treat should be analyzed to make sure it isn't something that is a bad influence and would send you back into your old ways.

Finding Your Personal Mission

Finding your personal mission if you have not already is

not as hard as you may think. Chances are you have already found your personal mission, yet you have never actually identified it because it comes so naturally to you and it may not stand out as anything significant or special. In many cases, people find that their personal missions are things that they have already been into or committed to for their life, yet they are so used to being committed to this mission that it does not stand out to them. For that reason, finding your personal mission is typically more focused on reflection than it is on actually going out and finding something to be committed to.

How to Set Effective Goals

When you set effective goals, you give your mind a sense of safety by showing yourself that there is a clear path for you to be talking and that it leads you to where you want to go. For people who find themselves engaging in procrastination due to uncertainty, this leads to them resolving the primary reason why they are not advancing so that they can begin to proceed toward their goals with confidence.

Understanding Your Personal "Why"

Developing your personal "why" is not unlike developing a purpose for your business or your business goals if you are an entrepreneur. It starts by identifying what your purpose is and identifying what the beliefs are that are driving you forward in achieving the goal that you have set out to achieve. A great way to understand what your why is meant to answer is to ask yourself these questions:

"WHY are you alive right now?"

"WHY were you inspired to get out of bed this morning?"

"WHY should people care about this?"

These types of question help give your personal mission meaning and significance, and while it does not need to be developed to please anyone else, considering how you justify the significance of your personal mission can help you identify why it matters. Your "why" statement sets you apart from everyone else and gives you a strong motivation to move ahead in life and steadily work toward what you want to achieve.

Measuring Your Personal Progress

A large part of self-discipline is self-awareness, so naturally, it is important that you invest time in learning how to measure your personal progress so that you can begin developing an awareness of how well you are advancing down your chosen path. Learning how to measure your personal progress will help you determine what it is that you need to focus more on, and where you are doing great.

Creating a Winner Effect

Creating a winner effect starts by understanding that you are more likely to achieve your bigger goals if you first achieve your smaller goals. This is why having milestones on the way to your goals is helpful: each one can be celebrated as its own goal and makes you far more likely to achieve your larger goals in the long run.

Rewarding Yourself

When you reward yourself, make sure to combine delayed gratification with a reward that is big enough to make it worth it. So, the longer the gratification is delayed and the bigger the size of your goal, the larger your reward should be for yourself. This way, your brain sees that the longer you wait and the more you achieve, the more you win in the long run. You can reward yourself effectively by determining what your reward will be in advance and then using that to stay inspired to remain on track with your goal, thus allowing you to continue working toward your goals in a way that embodies self-discipline.

Using Commitment Devices

There are many valuable commitment devices that you can begin using to help you commit to self-discipline in your life if you truly want to recruit additional support to keep you on track. Commitment devices are generally a tool that you use to keep yourself on track with a commitment, either by rewarding yourself for a job well done or punishing yourself for not remaining on track with your commitment.

Making Marginal Gains

One great way for you to master self-discipline is to learn the art of making marginal gains. The idea of marginal gains is similar to the idea that stimulates the winner effect: marginal gains build your confidence and keep you feeling like you can genuinely create the type of success that you desire, which builds your momentum and keeps you moving forward. When it comes to marginal gains, rather than focusing on achieving goals that you already know that you can achieve, you want to focus on creating goals for yourself that stretch you slightly beyond what you are already achieving right now.

Managing Your Personal Energy

A person who has truly mastered self-discipline does not only know how to schedule their time according to their natural sleep-wake cycle but also knows how to manage their energy by making the most of it and learning how to increase their energy as needed. This way, the self-disciplined individual can develop enough energy to get things done and allot the right amount of energy to the right tasks, thus allowing them to accomplish even more in their life.

Protecting Your Time

A person with self-discipline will not only keep their schedule well-organized, but they will also be very mindful to avoid doing anything that could become a waste of time. In their opinion, time is a precious and limited resource and there is nothing worse than having it wasted.

Shaping Your Environment

Shaping your environment to keep you on track means

removing any and all distractions that may prevent you from staying focused, eliminating temptations, and adding elements to your environment that make staying on track easier. You can do this by decluttering, removing any objects that promote unwanted activities or habits, and adding items that promote wanted activities. This way, your environment is ready for you to succeed in and you are more likely to get everything done.

Surrounding Yourself with the Right People

If you want to adjust your behavior and master self-discipline, surround yourself with people who are also focused on mastering self-discipline and being conscious and mindful of their behaviors. When you surround yourself with people who have the same goals and desires as you do, you make it easier for you to actually stay on track because you are no longer surrounded by people who behave as temptations themselves.

Being Kind with Yourself

Self-discipline is truly a path of self-mastery, which means understanding yourself at a deeper level and understanding how to push yourself to excellence without pushing yourself to the breaking point. Your goal here is to understand that fine line between where you can perform at peak effort and where you are starting to push yourself too far. Being kind with yourself is not just about knowing when to quit either; it can come in many different ways.

Being kind to yourself is an opportunity to get to know yourself more and to get to like yourself more, and so you can engage in kindness as a part of your personal mission so that you can really develop your relationship with yourself and get to know how your inner operating system works.

Chapter 16: How to Develop Self-Discipline?

Self-discipline is the ability to look at your true desires and determine that the outcomes at the end of your goals are much worthier and more enjoyable than your current impulses and distractions and sticking with it long enough to make it through hard situations. Recognizing any area, you need to improve is always the first step to creating a plan. Otherwise, these will sneak up and sabotage your efforts. Self-discipline is driven by changing your habits, and truly the goal of discipline is a byproduct of the changes you make in habits, routines and daily activities.

Motivation

Your why and what motivates you can come from many areas, including internal and external. Your reasons can include how it might make you feel, or other's feel but also what it can bring to your life. Money, stability, and a better job may be external reasons to work hard for a new job, but often they also bring internal factors like the peace that comes from financial stability or less stress from working as many hours.

Temptation

Remove any temptations like food, unhealthy activities, and build in positive rewards. Most of us do well when we are able to be rewarded when we perceive we are sacrificing something like comfort, enjoyable food or time spent doing something fun.

Reward

Make a list of things that you enjoy, even rewards that have nothing to do with your project or goal. For example, even if you are eating healthy, you can add in a reward that for every hour of studying you can have a small treat. Portion out those treats so that you also mitigate any temptation to binge.

Routine

Routines are one great way to allow us to reduce stress but also increase the pleasure principles that often drive procrastination. If we know that positive feelings drive our emotions, then we need to remember this value and create a predictable, stress-reducing and enjoyable routine that allows us to stick to our plans, not get confused about what happens next, and feels positive as well as soothing.

Healthy Living: Exercise, Eating, and Rest

Even if your actual goal isn't about health and wellness, eating right and exercising have multiple benefits to reducing procrastination and increasing your ability to be disciplined. People who take their goals seriously are also dedicated to pushing through things that may not be enjoyable at the moment for the positive ending benefit, like completing a hard workout because it is good for the body, or eating foods that are good for your body that may not taste as good as candy.

People who tend to be able to stick to goals do so in many

areas of their life, not just one. Since the major components of discipline involve pushing through discomfort, then applying that skill to health, work and relationships is natural. The ability to stick to what you want to accomplish even when the current moment isn't enjoyable means being willing to stick to a healthy routine of eating and working out.

One change in your life can ripple into other areas of your life. A commitment to exercise seems to have the largest impact in ability to persevere to a goal. It increases fitness and mental abilities, improves mood and impulse control, reduces weight, and reduces chances to get sick. Sticking to an exercise plan increases our ability to commit and stick to it.

It's always advisable to pick something you love to do and stick to doing that activity. If you hate running, don't run! If you love to dance, find a dance class! Exercise and goal setting never must look like anyone else's type of fitness, and everyone can move and feel better. If you've avoided it because you don't enjoy at the treadmill or lifting weights, start with any kind of movement that will motivate you and keep you going.

Eating for good energy is what creates a longer-lasting energy source and is good for the brain. Protein fuels the brain and body and helps to avoid energy crashes and hormone fluctuations because of carbohydrates. Leafy greens, healthy proteins, and lots of water are healthy sources of energy for your brain and body.

Outside of positive health benefits, engaging in something that keeps you active also keeps your brain active. Engaging in exercise does not give time for your negative thoughts to crop up and take root. Ensuring that you are not idle means you no longer have time for the brain to drift to the sabotaging thoughts. When you stay active, you simply don't have time to think about the things that can go wrong or reasons you shouldn't finish a task. And once you complete your task of exercise, the rest of your list seems to be possible.

Exercise also releases positive feel-good hormones like

endorphins. These can be a natural antidepressant, and the release of endorphins can be slow-releasing, long-lasting throughout your day, long after the exercise is over.

Ensuring that you have enough rest is key to having the energy for the next day. Rest and repair from effort today prepares you for the task ahead tomorrow. A well-rested mind and body can concentrate and engage in activities better. This is another area where routine and commitment pays off in creating a continuous loop. This is also a great time to meditate if you aren't in the habit yet of doing this in the morning.

Gratitude

Sometimes in the quest for a change in our lives, we tend to look at our current situations and decide that because we desire change, our circumstances as they are today being not worthy or desirable. In truth, if we harness the ability to separate those two, we are less prone to negative thinking. If you can remind yourself that you have parts of your life that are desirable and good, and you also simply want to meet new goals, your goals now no longer become a reflection of your life, as if you must meet your goals only and solely because your current life is not good enough.

Meditation: The Art of Disciplining Your Mind

The practice of meditation and mindfulness has the power to increase your willpower. Meditation and mindfulness both use the art of staying present in the moment without being prone to distraction or needing to avoid emotion and serve to increase emotional awareness and intelligence.

Stress and anxiety are often the downfalls of completing goals, and often, these bring negative thoughts about ourselves that create a negative feedback loop. Meditation works to notice when those are happening and cancel them out. It releases feel-good chemicals, just like exercise that can help reduce the stress hormones like cortisol that feed anxiety. Meditation and mindfulness reduce cravings and the desire to act on impulses by calming the very hormones that feed those.

Using Affirmations

Affirmations are seeking positive observances and being grateful. Affirmations are always self-focused and are positive or neutral challenges to any negative self-talk.

"Today, I choose to commit to myself and my own happiness and whatever it takes to get there."

"Today, I choose not to engage in self-sabotaging behaviors."

"I have all the energy and direction I need to accomplish my desired goals."

The words that we say out loud or even internally are not reality. However, whatever we perceive to be the truth is a reality for ourselves and we will act as if these things are true. We see ourselves and the world around us through the lens of our thoughts, and if those are negative, we are then prone to see the world in that same way.

The way we talk to ourselves matters and without motivation from within in the form of positive affirmations and encouragements, we are doomed to tell ourselves that we will fail and that will become our truth. Positive people and mentors are helpful at catching negative talk and helping us correct that, but our most positive influence should always be ourselves.

The interesting thing about affirmations is that they themselves are a form of discipline. Just like engaging in healthy eating and exercise, this is a type of dedication, that if done daily, results in an improvement in a discipline in other areas of life.

Organization and Time Management

An organized operational life is a disciplined approach to life. If you are totally overwhelmed starting with your goals, then start with something physical in your space that you can organize. You may discover that you need an organized external life to focus yourself internally and avoid procrastination.

Commitment

Commitment to a goal or plan is a choice and is a step towards discipline. The difference in commitment and learning discipline is that there are no anxiety or negative emotions with commitment. You simply choose the action or plan and decide to continue that daily.

Don't Be a Perfectionist

Forgiving yourself and simply noticing where you can make changes, from a natural perspective, is much healthier and keeps you on task much longer. Accomplishing big things doesn't usually follow a simple straight line. Mistakes are also learning opportunities instead of failures. Learning from each of your mistakes and making new commitments to change continue to build self-discipline.

Chapter 17: Creating a Support Network

Success doesn't happen alone. In fact, most success stories depend on a rally of friends and family who were all able to help keep the succeeding person on track. There are always several factors that contribute to changing behaviors and meeting goals, but personal improvement because of positive people really cannot be minimized.

It never hurts to have people cheering you on! We know from research that people who attempt marathons are more likely to complete the run if there are supportive cheerleaders along the way, even if this isn't their first time to run.

Positive influencers aren't always necessarily those who simply cheer you on and give you nothing but positive feedback. In fact, sometimes they are the ones who push you the hardest and might give you the most criticism. Helpful criticism of course, but the direct observance of things you must change nonetheless!

Those who will help you stay accountable don't always make things feel good, but since they also have the eye on the end goal that you've proclaimed you want, they assist you in not going towards that short term, feel-good impulses and direct you back towards the harder efforts that will pay off in the end.

Positive people are often not jealous of your successes and will cheer you on, even if you surpass them in happiness, relationships, or income. These people are the ones who are the most supportive towards achieving your goals. They are ok helping you feel good about yourself and your plans, because they focus the same efforts towards themselves and life in general.

To succeed in meeting those daily and weekly tasks, you must have confidence that the amount of work and sacrifice will pay off. Sometimes that also includes putting yourself out there to make big changes that can rattle your friends and family. By nature, we as humans are averse to risk and we enjoy things that seem stable and routine. Supportive people can see your changes and risks, and they give you supportive encouragement instead of tearing down your plans because it makes them uncomfortable. Positive people recognize that not all change is risky and that not all risk is something to avoid.

Chapter 18: Strengthen Your Willpower

Willpower is the distinguishing ability that enables you to exercise power over or to influence you will positively. Willpower allows you to resist harmful impulses and stick to an informed decision.

Willpower and self-discipline are often used interchangeably, but they are not the same. Although both qualities are essential because they work together towards helping you to accomplish your goals, they have distinct differences. Willpower is the exertion when you are determined to accomplish a task. It is the level of control that individual use to restrain their impulses.

Willpower can be short-lived and only used when the moment calls for it. Sometimes, it could be as simple as following a set of temporary rules to achieve a short-term result, like dieting or quitting smoking. In short, it is the ability to push and control yourself and your actions when needed.

Self-discipline, on the other hand, is about your mindset. It is focused on getting in touch with yourself, what you want, what you believe in and shaping your life around that belief. Self-discipline is a trait that is built for life. There is no short-term solution or rules to be followed. It is a quality that is built for a lifetime. Willpower can help you do just that.

Willpower is a powerful tool that can help you dominate your life and enhance self-discipline. However, caution is advised. You need to know that your willpower differs depending on the time of day and circumstances. When you are tired and stressed out, your willpower is usually at its lowest.

When you fortify your willpower, you will be able to stand strong and accomplish your objectives even when circumstances are not that favorable. The good news is that despite what many people think, willpower can be strengthened without exerting too much effort.

Let us look at how you can do this:

Build Your Pressure Capacity

It starts with the little things like resisting that voice that tells you to resist doing something until the next day. As the popular saying goes, "tomorrow never comes." There are always other tomorrows, and thus, if you keep postponing what you need to do, you may end up never doing it. Stop postponing. Stop procrastinating. Little by little, you will be able to fortify your willpower. Additionally, because you've enhanced your capacity for pressure, you will be able to exercise your willpower even when you need to make difficult decisions.

Calm Negative Emotions

When you fortify your willpower, you take charge of your emotions, actions, and reactions. Notice that although the emotions are still there, what changes are how you react despite having them. You need to be on the lookout for things such as anger, boredom, and tiredness among others. This is because when you experience powerful emotions, your judgment is usually clouded. This is why you need to still and calm such emotions.

Manage Inner Conflict

Experiencing inner conflict is common since we are constantly making decisions, or we have to take action. One voice pulls you this way and the other that way. You may want to do something, but somehow, you convince yourself that doing it is not worth the effort.

Meditate

Meditation is good for the brain. When you meditate, the gray matter in your brain builds up. The gray matter is responsible for regulating emotions. Also, it is where decision making takes place. This is why meditation is great for your willpower. It enables you to make decisions without the interference of emotions. The act of meditating itself requires discipline. Meditation fosters willpower and leads to personal improvement.

Exercise

Everybody knows that exercise is beneficial. However, few people religiously follow an exercise regime. The main reason for this is that people view exercise as a tedious job. They find excuses not to start it, and thus, they never reach the point where exercising becomes routine. However, it is vital that you embrace exercise. Exercise is linked to enhanced mental performance and improved willpower.

Get Enough Sleep

The human body needs sleep in order to rejuvenate itself. This is why sleep deprivation is dangerous. It wreaks havoc on the prefrontal cortex. This area helps control cravings and your response to stress. When you have adequate rest, you give your brain the energy it needs to do its work well.

Focus on "Later"

Willpower calls for taking charge of your actions and emotions. Unfortunately, sometimes, this is not easy, especially if you have a bad habit you want to get rid of. Intense cravings are hard to ignore especially since you know you won't even have that thing you were used to.

Be Accountable

Accountability is a word that means a lot. It causes people to pause and think about the consequences of what they are about to do. When you are accountable to others, you strive to behave in a manner that will not cause them distress or displeasure. You would also not want to let such people down.

Have Self-Belief

When you are talking about self-belief, always remember that the keyword is self. Self-belief is that strong conviction you have that gives you confidence that you can accomplish what you set your mind to. In life, you will find it difficult to unleash your potential if you don't believe in yourself. A self-belief is an interesting tool. It can be sharpened or dampened by others but ultimately, you need to make up your mind about it.

Mark Your Starting Point

The first thing you need to acknowledge is where you are when it comes to believing in yourself. This is the point where you need to honestly search your deepest thoughts and feelings. Note down your feelings on different aspects of your life. Are you living your ideal life? If not, what is holding you back from achieving what you want? Think of the limiting beliefs you possess and trace where they came from. Did they come from someone else or were they conceived due to past experiences? Once you know how you view yourself, you will be in an excellent position to adjust your view and improve yourself.

Quiet the Negative Inner Voice

Your inner thoughts, whether positive or negative, are

always present with you. They can be loud, or they can be quiet depending on how much attention you give them. You need to know that having negative thoughts is not a crime.

Turn Weaknesses to Strengths

One of the things that can limit your belief in yourself is your perceived weakness. Many people don't want others to be aware of their weaknesses. In fact, many would rather suffer silently than let others know of their struggles. However, self-belief is not a false belief in your abilities. It is not about presenting a perfect front. You need to acknowledge where you fall short and figure out how you can turn those weaknesses into strengths. Self-belief gives you the freedom to pursue your goals even in the face of opposition and limitations.

Develop Useful Traits

A weakness that you can correct is one that requires knowledge or skills. As long as you are capable of it, you can learn a new skill. You don't have to be clueless when it comes to a skill that may be useful to you. You need to learn all you can about something you are dealing with. This will boost your confidence and belief that you can indeed tackle any situation that arises in the course of you doing your job.

Re-imagine Yourself

Focus on the new you that you've created and seen yourself transforming into that person. This way, you will be able to remove yourself from a position of helplessness to that of power and self-belief. When you re-imagine yourself, you will have the needed motivation to work towards achieving your goals. Ensure that you visualize what being a new you will achieve and how it will make you feel. The more desirous the benefits, the more you will work to achieve your goal.

We all have great willpower; you just need to show yourself that. Well, with these exercises you can easily begin the journey to making that kind of proof available to yourself. With greater willpower comes the ability to improve your overall self-discipline.

Chapter 19: Self-Discipline Is Simply Self-Control.

It is the power to avoid unhealthy excesses in life, as well as upholding perseverance, determination, endurance, and restraint before action. It is completing what you began along with the ability to work on implementing decisions. Self-discipline is about fulfilling objectives despite obstacles and hardships. One of the fundamental traits about self-discipline is to sacrifice instant gratification or pleasure in exchange for higher gains.

Improve Your Self-Control

One-way self-discipline manifests itself is in the way you are able to resist temptation and overcome bad habits. Self-control plays a major role in this. If you cannot control your words, your thoughts and your actions, you will find it increasingly difficult to dominate your life and improve yourself. As such, it is important to gain self-control.

You can do the below things to improve your self-control.

Identify what you want to control

When talking about self-control, people often don't discuss what it is they want to control. Many just talk of self-control in general. However, self-control needs to be channeled to a particular purpose or thing. You can control some things but doing so will be detrimental to your health.

Do your research

Once you are aware of what you need to control, you need to embark on research to understand more about your subject. You can go a step further by learning how to communicate and assert yourself without giving in to anger. The more you learn about the behavior you want to control, the better you'll become at controlling it and the more you become self-disciplined.

Set realistic goals

Self-control takes time to develop. You need to set realistic goals especially if you are trying to resist something you are used to giving into. This is especially true for those who want to quit harmful habits such as smoking. In such a case, it is not enough to say that you want to quit smoking. You need to set goals and establish strategies that will enable you to be successful in your quest. You will have to look at the challenges you will encounter.

Monitor your progress

Self-control is not just about learning to get rid of bad habits. It is also about not giving in to temptation. When you have self-control, you will desist from things such as overdrinking, heavy eating, getting into debt, and cheating. These things have varying consequences but are harmful nonetheless. Strengthening your self-control involves you visualizing different scenarios and determining how the scenarios will play out.

Know when to seek help

Seeking help is not a weakness but rather a show of strength. In essence, you will be showing that you are willing to take control back by using the available means to work on your problems and overcome your issues. Talking to a trusted friend, a religious leader, or a professional counsel will help you regain control.

Create a support system

Never underestimate the value of a support system. It is not human nature to live in isolation. Sometimes all it takes is seeing a friendly face for you to feel like your world is right again. Surrounding yourself with friends and family will be good for you. Many individuals find comfort in group support.

Develop Positive Habits

Self-discipline is all about managing your actions and controlling your reactions. The actions you perform every day have more often than not become habits. When you develop positive habits, it becomes easier to be self-disciplined because you don't have to concentrate so much on managing your actions and reactions since you are used to positive habits.

Determine what you want

There is no way you can motivate yourself to do something if you have no idea what that something is. You need to channel your efforts and the only way to do this effectively is by determining what you want. Make it a habit to look at situations objectively.

Know your competition

There is no doubt that self-discipline helps you achieve your goals and improve yourself. However, when it comes to what you want to achieve in life and the qualities you want to develop, you may start comparing yourself to others. It is one thing to admire the achievements of someone, but it is another thing to focus all your efforts on becoming like that individual. You need to acknowledge that you are your own competition. You are the one who determines what your standards are. You are the one who knows whether you've met your own standards. This is why you need to focus on your own improvement. Your goal should be to always take positive steps instead of backsliding.

Celebrate small victories

As it has been said, it takes time to master self-discipline. Circumstances and situations can cause you to take a bad step. Other times it may seem like you've achieved nothing. This can often be discouraging. Thus, it is important that you learn to recognize and celebrate small victories. Small victories alert you to the fact that you are not a helpless case. When you are trying to improve your life, you start by making small strides. However, if you don't take time to bask in your achievements, you may lose sight of your goals. The other good thing about celebrating small victories is that it motivates you to stay your course.

Get inspired by others

One thing that often leads to discouragement is the thought that you cannot successfully achieve what you plan to achieve. That feeling makes tasks seem larger than life. It hampers productivity and keeps you from dominating your life. However, if you find out that others have been in your shoes and come out successful, you will be more inclined to continue improving yourself. Inspiring stories and quotes are all over the internet and in books. Your friend or your family member can give you the inspiration you need to change your life.

Eliminate stress

Eliminating stress lightens your mood and gives you the energy, motivation, and freedom to pursue self-improvement. You need to find a way to de-stress. This may mean talking it out with a friend, taking a warm bath and watching a comedy, or simply taking a nature walk. Find out what works for you and include it in your schedule.

Have fun

Sometimes it's not the task you do but the method you use to do it that determines your rate of success. Take the example of exercise, for instance. Many people complain that exercising is too difficult. It seems so formal and structured. However, many people who complain about exercise have no problem participating in activities such as dancing or taking a walk. They don't realize that they can choose to do a physical activity they enjoy for their workout. When you introduce fun to an activity, you begin to look forward to doing it.

Filter your information intake

Information seems to be everywhere nowadays. There are countless television stations, blogs, and books out there. The motto of the day seems to be that everyone is an expert. This can drain you as you try to take in everything you can in order not to miss a thing. Well, you need to pause for a minute and determine how much information you will be taking in. There is only so much research you can do, after which you need to stop doing research and work on the knowledge you've gained.

Don't fear failure

Some people don't even try to achieve things simply because they fear failure. When you dwell on the possibility of failure, you begin to make potential difficulties stand out and this disheartens you even before you can try something. You need to put failure in perspective. If you fail to do something, you have the opportunity to learn what went wrong and adjust so that you can do better the next time. Failure does not define you. It just points out that you are human.

Don't fear success

Some people hold back, not because they fear failure, but because they fear success. However, what they don't realize is that they have already succeeded in many things in life. Attaining self-discipline will only prepare you to succeed in various areas of your life. If you fear success, ask yourself where that fear stems from. This way, you will be able to deal with the issues that crop up.

Make each day count

When it comes to self-discipline, you need to make each day count. The thing you need to understand the most is that self-discipline allows you to dominate your life and control your actions. This means that as long as you have self-discipline, you are in charge of your life. This is a powerful position that will have you leading a fulfilling life. You can ensure that you continue developing self-discipline by regulating yourself.

Invest in Self-Regulation

Self-regulation entails determining your deepest values and acting in a manner that will keep those values intact. It is closely related to self-discipline, as you need to dominate your life in order to act and react in a manner that will befit you. Self-regulation monitors whether or not you are on the right path as far as self-discipline is concerned.

Chapter 20: Tips to Build Self-Discipline

Don't Procrastinate

Procrastination gets you nowhere. It hampers productivity and ensures that you don't pursue positive habits. You need to discipline yourself to avoid procrastination. Get your priorities listed and set goals to improve your life. Take the time to note down the various ways you procrastinate.

Shun Excuses

Excuses seek to limit how far you can go. When you find excuses, you are essentially telling yourself that what you're dealing with is beyond your control. Thus, you will see that as a legitimate reason to not even bother trying.

Stand Firm

If you are indecisive or if you tend to follow the crowd, you will have a difficult time exercising self-discipline. Self-discipline is about controlling your actions. If you cannot make decisions, someone else will gladly step in to control your life. In order to avoid this, learn to evaluate situations and make objective decisions. You can be assertive without being disrespectful. And when your decisions are born from the knowledge and evidence you possess, you will have firmer grounds to stand on.

Determine Goals

The first element of success that we need to consider is being able to determine goals successfully. As a major element of success in general, learning to determine goals means putting into action a long-term plan. To avoid this problem in the future, you have to make up some actual goals to aim for. Everything else we'll be discussing needs solid and achievable goals around it for it to be a possibility. If you determine your goals today, then your overall discipline will begin to improve.

Devise a Plan of Action

Now, we have to work out how to make these goals a realistic possibility. What you need to do, then, is come up with a genuine long-term plan of action. A plan of action is so important to make sure that you can reach your potential as a person. We have goals to follow, so now we need to start actively planning and preparing your plan of action for each. Every goal needs to have a genuine plan waiting for it at the end that can be used to make that goal a possibility.

Creating the Plans

The easiest ways to manage a plan of action is simply to begin researching. Let's say that you want to try and run your own business but lack the discipline to start the process. Your first goal should be to work out the feasibility of setting up that business in your own area.

Prioritize Tasks

Task prioritization means that we can ensure that our plan of action and our goals are running alongside each other. As we mentioned before, the main goal should be to put your tasks in chronological order.

Visualize Success

The ability to see yourself doing something is a great way to stay disciplined. We lose discipline when we lose faith in our chances of succeeding at something – anything. If you want to avoid this kind of negative downturn in thinking, then you have to be able to properly visualize what is to come. The reason for doing this is quite simple – when you visualize success, you feel easier about the reality of it happening.

Develop Self-Awareness

A bit of self-awareness can go a long way when it comes to keeping your discipline. Having self-awareness means that you are far more alert to your role in both success and failure. Those who are self-aware can see their own limitations and flaws and are less defensive when someone actually points them out.

Eat Right

If you eat right, then you give your body the nutrition that it needs to run properly and thus make success more likely. If you eat right, too, you make sure that you have the energy to get through those sapping days. When a problem comes up that tests your discipline, eating right can help you get through that problem.

Exercise Right

If you start to exercise right, then you give your body an immense lesson: that it can deal with challenges. That you can overcome personal problems. That you are able to fight back. Many of us find it pretty tough to get to that stage but when you do, self-discipline becomes far easier to get a hold of and actively control.

Morning Routine

Discipline means making sure that your life has a very

specific style and routine to it – and this is no different from having a morning routine. If you can make sure that your mornings are more balanced and have a specific plan to them, then the rest of the day can fall into place. It creates a uniform nature in your mind that takes away the uncertainty at the beginning of the day. By doing this you become far more likely to reach specific targets throughout the day and thus are more likely to be where you want to be, come to the end of the day.

Practice Self-Control

Self-control is such a vital skill that many of us never bother to investigate or use it properly. We all just believe that we have it — but practicing self-control can be such a therapeutic skill. If you want to make sure that your day can go ahead smoothly and that you can retain your discipline, you need a more effective level of self-control or your day will just spiral into confusion.

Control Your Finances

Let's speak again about the importance of having domination over your finances and your overall financial command. By learning to control your finances, then you can make it much, much easier to control other aspects of your life. Let's say you are looking to make your life easier by having financial control so that you can begin to invest in a long-term business idea.

Find Your Mission

We all have a mission in our lives, and the hardest part of maintaining any form of self-discipline comes from finding your mission. If you don't know what these goals and targets we spoke of are supposed to achieve, you'll never get anywhere!

Find What Fulfills You

Take the time to really consider every element of what will

fulfill you. Is it a personal success? Fame and attention? Financial security? Helping others? Shining a light on a particular issue? Whatever the aims and reasons are, you'll find that what fulfills you can be easily understood if you head down a particular route. To find out what is going to make you feel happiest and most secure, you simply have to start believing and understanding in your own personal beliefs.

This is the most powerful part of self-discipline. When you are doing what you believe is the right thing, very little can slow you down or limit your chances of being a genuine success.

Ignore Naysayers

When you are trying to stand firm and practice self-discipline, you should not be surprised to face opposition. However, you need not succumb to naysayers. You can learn to ignore them. First, determine whether what they are saying is valid. Sometimes people tell you well-meaning things in a hurtful manner without intending to. Sieve through the words to see areas in which you can make improvements and use the criticism to improve yourself.

Have the End in Sight

It is vital that you have the end in sight at all times. Of course, you don't want to be so caught up in the end product that you forget to work on the process. However, it would help to remember what you are working towards. This way, even when things get difficult, you will have the needed self-discipline to keep going.

Limit Distractions

Distractions come in many forms. Few people have the luxury to work in solitude. Every now and then, you may find someone poking in to check up on you or someone stopping by to chat with you because they are bored. You may also find yourself answering phone calls and checking email. You need to know beforehand how you will deal with such distractions. This is because you may find yourself wasting a lot of time on things that lessen productivity. Limiting distractions is part of self-discipline.

Finish What You Start

You need to promise yourself that you will finish whatever you start. If you make it a habit to finish projects, you will gain the self-discipline needed to improve your life for the better. Half-finished projects are a sign of disorganization and a lack of motivation. Start by finishing smaller projects as soon as you start them. This way, you will be in a better position to complete other projects that need your attention.

Chapter 21: Exploring the Concepts of Accountability and Honesty

What happens when we lack accountability and honesty with ourselves is that we begin to get into cycles where nothing changes? We increase our bad habits, we drive them deeper into our subconscious, and we procrastinate making any changes because we have yet to admit or even recognize the fact that we are our own problem.

If you want to start making serious changes in your life, you need to be willing to learn how you can hold yourself accountable and how you can start being honest with yourself.

To become honest and accountable with yourself is more than just an act of self-discipline, it is an act of self-love. As you can see, there are many reasons why you need to begin to become accountable to yourself and stay honest with yourself, so that you can begin increasing your sense of self-awareness and truly taking steps toward making a change in your life.

Becoming accountable and honest with yourself starts by being willing to admit that you are imperfect. You need to be willing to accept that you are going to make mistakes and that implementing changes in your life is not going to happen overnight. You are going to have to put in the effort and continue working toward making these shifts so that you can see the effects of them, which means that there are going to be days where you are successful in making your shifts, and there are days where you struggle. Being willing to admit to yourself when you are struggling, addressing, and assessing why you are struggling will help you determine whether it was just an off day, or if you need to make some adjustments in your approach to what you are attempting to accomplish.

If you are not used to being accountable and honest with yourself, keeping a journal is a great opportunity for you to begin practicing. A journal can provide you with the opportunity to check in with yourself in regards to your changes on a daily basis, allowing you to rate how well you feel you did and whether or not you feel like you need to make any shifts. This way, you can continually recheck your new habits or desired behaviors and encourage yourself to stay honest and accountable. If you find that staying accountable to the journal itself is a challenge because you are particularly resistant around accountability practices, using a reminder on your phone can be a great start to shift this behavior.

Accountability and honesty sound so simple, but they are among the most difficult self-discipline components to master. It is natural to not want to face failures and negative feelings, so having to be accountable and honest can be hard.

Being honest with yourself means that you are able to admit your shortcomings as they occur. It also means that you can adequately congratulate yourself when you do overcome a challenge and experience success.

Being more accountable means that you are able to take responsibility for the choices that you make. For example, if you give into a bad habit, you immediately recognize this and take the steps to prevent it from happening again.

Both accountability and greater honesty with yourself are skills that you can learn, with some work. The first step is to determine how honest and accountable you currently are so that you know where work needs to be done.

Being more honest with yourself is hard. There is no other way to put it. It is not something that you can just start doing overnight, nor is it innate. Part of being honest with yourself is also making sure that you are more honest with other people, as the two concepts go hand in hand.

The good news is that you can improve your overall level of honesty. There are certain tips that you can start putting into practice now to help you. Just know that it takes time, so you have to keep at it to get the best results.

Using Honesty and Accountability to Improve Self-Discipline

When you are working on your self-discipline, it is important that you exercise both accountability and honesty. Now that you know what they are and how to exercise them, you will be able to easily work them into your strategy for greater self-discipline.

It is a good idea to start with being more honest with yourself. This is because it makes it possible for you to identify your bad habits. It is imperative that you are honest about all of your bad habits; even those that you only engage in occasionally; each must be identified and replaced with a good habit.

The accountability will play into your ability to change your bad habits. You will need to keep a check on the changes that you are making. You also need to be able to recognize when you might be slipping and allowing your bad habits to creep back into your life. Use the accountability strategies above to help with this part of the process since it will make it easier to craft an effective accountability plan.

Once you completely reverse a bad habit, you have to maintain your honesty and accountability. Once a bad habit has been established, even after you overcome it, there is always a chance that you can adopt it again or fall into a new one, so be vigilant.

Chapter 22: Procrastination and How to Get It under Control

You know what procrastination is, but do you realize how much of an impact it has on your life? Most people do not see the negative effects of their procrastination each day. However, the truth is that if you are procrastinating, you will never achieve the highest level of self-discipline possible.

To put it simply, procrastination involves doing tasks that are less urgent, or completely unimportant, instead of taking care of your most important responsibilities. In some cases, people choose to do pleasurable things instead of taking care of their responsibilities.

Why Procrastination Kills Self-Discipline

You can see that procrastination can take over your life and cause a wealth of issues that can be difficult to solve once they start to occur. One area of your life that it can have a profound effect on is your self-discipline.

In order for you to be self-disciplined, you have to get tasks done as needed. If you procrastinate, this is impossible. It destroys your productivity level and makes it impossible to keep up with your responsibilities.

Before you can even begin to work on enhancing your self-discipline, you must overcome procrastination. If you do not, your goals will be dead in the water before you even start.

It is no secret or surprise that procrastination can prevent you from accomplishing many things in life. Procrastination can prevent people from finding a job, finishing a diploma, calling a friend, cleaning their house, or even going out for a walk or getting some exercise in. Some people are low-grade procrastinators, in that they will procrastinate the bigger things but are always on target with smaller things.

Drawing the conclusion around how procrastination is killing your self-discipline is easy: you want to be doing things that are more productive toward achieving your goals, but instead, you are doing everything else. When it comes to learning how to become self-disciplined, if you are more concerned with your television show or hanging out with your friends over-exercising or personal development, guess what? You are going to be doing everything aside from what actually serves you in advancing toward the goals that you have set for yourself.

How to Overcome Procrastination

What is nice about overcoming procrastination is that with the right strategy and amount of work, it is something that everyone is able to do. The following are common techniques used to tackle procrastination and get it out of your life for good:

- Take your task and break it down into smaller steps.
- Make sure to change your environment into a space that does not allow for procrastination.
- Make sure you always have specific deadlines and a detailed timeline for all of your responsibilities.
- Identify your common procrastination "pit stops" and eliminate them from your life.
- Make sure that you are spending time with people who are self-disciplined and do not procrastinate, to keep you inspired.

- Tell people about your goals, because this will help to keep you more accountable.
- Find a buddy to help you to keep your eye on the prize.
- Take your goals and re-clarify them if you find yourself procrastinating on specific ones and you cannot figure out why.
- Find someone who has overcome procrastination in their life and make them your friend so that you have someone who can provide tips and information about this.
- See each task in the simplest manner possible, because if you over-complicate them, then you are more likely to want to avoid them since no one wants to work on overwhelming tasks.

Chapter 23: How to Maintain Self-Discipline When Facing Adversity and Challenges

Do you function with a deep-seated fear of failure that prevents you from chasing your dreams? You may have chanced upon some failures, disappointments, and disillusionment along the way and quit when a little more effort would have taken to your ultimate dream life.

It is easy to stay self-disciplined when things are going right. However, during adversity, it can be challenging to sustain your self-discipline levels. Our self-discipline is often tested during challenging times.

The rich and successful may not necessarily have it any easier than you or me if that is what you believe. Few things underline our success as much as our discipline and perseverance. The self-disciplined mindset is confident and believes in their abilities enough to sustain through tough times. Self-disciplined people realize that time is the most vital resource, and they optimize their time by investing in themselves.

The rich, wealthy, and successful master ace time-management skills and possess the knack for seizing challenges and converting adversities into opportunities. Successful people lead a disciplined, balanced, and controlled life by delaying gratification or pleasure for the larger picture.

The self-disciplined have a secure perception of themselves. They are proactive when it comes to viewing their failures, adversities, and circumstances. Winners understand that you can have a very powerful reason to do something or an excuse to give up. You just cannot have both. Successful people are indeed destined to succeed. It is only a matter of time before they achieve their real glory. When things get tough, they change the course of their action, but they will seldom give up or quit.

No individual is perfect. Even the rich and famous people we are in awe of have been through their share of trials to emerge winners. They have failed multiple times but never given up.

Accept your mistakes and assume responsibility for your actions instead of blaming other people or circumstances for them. When you accept responsibility for your actions, you take greater control of your life. When you accept your mistake, you realize that this is not the most suitable way to do something.

This will award you the power to overcome challenges. You will want to rise above your circumstances and situations. Every person you admire has at some point or another dealt with and overcome challenges that are responsible for their present success and glory.

As much as we would like to control things in life, some situations and challenges are going to be beyond our realm of control.

Chapter 24: Scheduling for Discipline

Self-discipline is one of the greatest virtues that a person can aim to obtain. There simply is not a single aspect of life where having self-discipline will not be beneficial. Self-discipline is the main ingredient to achieve success and fulfillment. Without self-discipline, you will always be at the whims and mercy of other people who do have self-discipline. It has often been said that the world is not fair. Whether that is true or not is irrelevant. If the world is not fair, then it is up to you to turn the tables in your own favor. If the world is fair, then it is also up to you to remain balanced and productive even when the odds start stacking against you.

During the worst of times, you will need the self-discipline to remain on your path instead of getting thrown off it. During the best of times, you will still need the self-discipline to remain centered and not become too presumptuous. If you lack discipline then you may give up on whatever you are trying to accomplish too early, or your ego may grow too big and trick you into falling into a bad habit. Practicing self-discipline gives you the power to keep going even when you are about to give up, as well as stop yourself before making too big of a mistake. It not only helps you to reach a higher platitude of success and fulfillment, but it also stops the bad judgment from manifesting as a bigger problem down the road.

The first pillar of self-discipline involves scheduling. In many ways, keeping a well-outlined schedule is the cornerstone of becoming, or remaining a disciplined person. There are many reasons why this is true. Having your activities set to the rhythm of a clock will help to establish good habits. At the end of the day, establishing and upholding good habits is what discipline truly aims to do. Your habits probably already, even if you don't realize it, are set to a schedule.

Keeping a solid schedule is the most efficient way of forcing good habits into your subconscious. This may sound ironic, but keeping a solid schedule is the first habit you will have to establish to cultivate self-discipline, and it is also the last. If you have a schedule of bad habits, then nothing will change. Yet, if you can create a schedule of good habits, then soon enough you won't even recognize the type of person you are anymore. The old you, unproductive and wasting time, will have transformed into a brand-new person who is capable of making their wildest dreams come true.

Before writing down your schedule and sticking to it, read through the rest of this book and then slowly arrange the schedule of your day. Scheduling, the cornerstone of self-discipline, is the first thing you have to understand before initiating the process of transformation. But it is also the last thing you have to work on. You have to know what good habits to include in your schedule before you can begin practicing them.

Chapter 25: Success Is a Process, Not a Moment of Glory

If you are serious in your pursuit of success, you need to have a realistic grasp of what it really entails. For most people, the term "success" conjures up an image of a winner celebrating their hard-earned achievement.

In fact, success is not a single achievement or even a series of achievements. It is an ongoing process. Successful people know that victory is a state of mind and actively cultivate it on a daily basis.

If you are guilty of magical or wishful thinking, you need to drop the habit fast if you are to master self-discipline and achieve anything of note. You are not exempt from the rules of the universe. If you want something, you are going to have to learn patience and find enjoyment in hard (and smart!) work.

This means that by daydreaming and half-heartedly planning what you want to happen instead of actively making your ambitions your reality, you are wasting precious time. When you appreciate just how much time it takes to attain and maintain any significant level of success, you won't be so willing to tolerate this mindset in either yourself or others. No one knows how much time they have left on this planet, and frittering it away is incredibly wasteful.

So how can you actually start putting your most cherished plans into practice? You'd be forgiven for thinking that motivation is the key to sustaining the energy required to work towards success over a long period of time. However, as you are about to discover in the next chapter, motivation isn't as magical as you might believe.

Why Negative Emotions Can Fuel Your Success

However positive you are and however well you may set yourself up for success, there will be times of despair, sadness, anger, and frustration. To be human is to experience a full spectrum of emotions. Most of us try and shy away from any kind of negative feelings. When we feel bad, we often try to forget about it as soon as possible and get back to feeling happy or at least "OK" as quickly as possible.

As long as you have come to accept that suffering is inevitable, you are ready to make good use of your unpleasant emotions. Negative feelings like sadness or despair are clear signals that something is wrong and needs to change. Think of your negative emotions not as inconveniences that need to be "solved," but rather as helpful signposts that highlight what steps you must take in order to improve your quality of life.

Instead of harnessing their negative emotions in a constructive manner and using them as an incentive to put together a plan of action, most people try and ignore uncomfortable feelings. Humans are emotion-driven creatures who gravitate towards drama, so you may as well make the most of your negative energy.

Some people find that the worst moments in their lives, such as losing a partner to an illness, can prompt them to succeed in ways they could never have imagined. The good news is that you can deal with shame and develop a healthier attitude.

Chapter 26: Delaying Gratification & Overcoming Temptation

How Instant Gratification Works Against You

Instant gratification is one natural behavioral tendency that virtually every human is wired to have. Instant gratification means that you are immediately rewarded for what you have engaged in. For example, if you are hungry and you go eat right away, you are immediately satisfied. Alternatively, if you post a new picture to Instagram or Facebook and immediately receive tons of new likes and comments, you are receiving instant gratification. The basis of survival has us leaning toward tendencies of instant gratification, because these behaviors allow us to immediately fulfill a need, such as eating or going to the bathroom.

For many people, the delay in gratification that we experience in society stimulates anxiety and discomfort. We find ourselves feeling unhappy or disappointed because we are not having our needs met immediately. For some people, this even triggers the development of actual anxiety disorders because they have not effectively learned how to naturally trigger their brain to engage in delayed gratification in a way that is not scary or uncomfortable. This can really develop a problem when it comes to gratification in general because the entire concept stimulates discomfort and misery for many people.

Anxiety and discomfort are not the only negative side effects of instant gratification, either. Instant gratification can lead to many unwanted side effects that can negatively impact your life and cause you to have unwanted outcomes in your life. In fact, instant gratification is one of the leading reasons for why many people do not have self-discipline mastered: because they are not yet capable of putting off their desired results until they have found a more effective and productive way to achieve them. This inability to gain gratification in a healthier way can lead to many behaviors that can cause troubles for a person.

Most of the time, the key reason why we give way to behaviors that make us feel and appear to be lazy or a procrastinator is that we do not feel like we are going to get gratification from doing something right away. We either want to gain the gratification right away, or we want a different type of gratification that the behavior we "should" be doing may not offer. In the end, we create negative and unwanted outcomes for ourselves because we are giving in to instant gratification and not considering or valuing the long-term outcome that our behaviors are creating.

How to Naturally Delay Gratification

The key to learning how to delay gratification is learning how to do it alongside your natural tendencies and desires. Learning how to delay gratification by identifying how you naturally do this and how you can do it in a more aligned manner ensures that you are working with your individual nature to create the results that you truly desire.

In addition to ensuring that you are operating in your own natural way, you can begin teaching yourself to delay gratification by first doing it in a small way, with things that do not have a huge impact.

The same sort of building-up-to-it process can be used for

virtually any type of changes you want to develop in your life. The more you add up to it by taking your time and slowly making the stakes higher and delaying the gratification longer, the more you are going to find yourself having an easy time with the delayed gratification. This is an excellent way to build yourself up to it so that your delayed gratification develops with ease and with a clear benefit that shows your brain that it is worth the investment.

Another great way to increase your gratification naturally is to become clear around what your values are and what you want to have and what you want to create in your life so that you are always operating in alignment with your own values. In many cases, delaying gratification and learning how to develop self-discipline in this area comes with mastering your mindset around your behaviors and ensuring that you are always behaving in a way that is relevant to what you truly care about. When you master your mindset around your values and begin to truly develop an inner sense of caring about what it is that you are creating in your life, it becomes easier for you to delay gratification.

Another great way that you can develop your delayed gratification abilities is by getting clear on what it is that you desire to create more of in your life and how you can create it. When you have a goal, a plan, and a clear focus, delayed gratification becomes easier because you are not attempting to follow an aimless path toward a nameless goal that will have unidentified results. Instead, you see exactly what it is that you are creating, how you are getting there, what you are getting as a result, and even when you can expect it by. For many people, having these questions answered makes delaying gratification easier because it removes the element of uncertainty, which is often what increases anxiety in people in the first place.

The best way to create a plan to support you with delaying gratification is to first identify how you are having your instant gratification fulfilled by your current actions. Pay attention to what specific needs or desires you are having fulfilled by these behaviors and why it is making you feel good or like you are receiving something positive out of it.

This is going to help you clearly identify what it is that you are attempting to gain and what you value in that particular situation so that you can continue to fulfill that specific goal, only in a more productive way.

Conclusion

Thank you for making it through to the end of this book. I hope it was able to help you learn more about self-discipline, building a success mindset, and practical strategies through which you can start practicing self-discipline in your life right away to accomplish the success, wealth, and glory that you are destined to accomplish.

Make sure that you remember that improving your self-discipline is a journey. It will not happen overnight, and this is a good thing. A slow progression will ensure that the positive changes that you are making will stick. This is because you will be developing them more naturally.

It is important to follow this book as it is written, since each chapter and part builds upon the ones before it. You will start by learning about your behavior and habits, and how they develop. This allows you to craft a natural and effective plan to make changes where they are needed.

Being self-disciplined implies several actions that are completely needed to build this value. You have read about having self-esteem and self-worth, being responsible, considerate, thoughtful, to practice forgiveness, being organized, being diligent, etc. This means that building self-discipline is not a hard task if you are really willing to be disciplined, but it has several things to take into account.

How many good opportunities have you had and lost just

because of a lack of self-discipline? Now you know that being disciplined, organized, trustworthy, and effective can be developed in easy ways. You just needed the willpower to improve your good habits and get rid of the bad ones. Now that you know more about self-discipline and how easy is to get there, you must be encouraged to have a personal and professional growth based on this essential value. You learned what you could lose for not having it (and you probably already have lost something due to that), the great benefits of being self-disciplined, and that one easy way to reaching your goals is by being disciplined, how to build discipline, and what ways you increase it through common activities.

The important role self-discipline plays in your life goes a long way to justify every effort and time you put into building your self-discipline. The techniques outlined in this book will guide you on this self-discipline journey to enable you to live a better and more meaningful life.

www.ingramcontent.com/pod-product-compliance
Lightning Source LLC
Chambersburg PA
CBHW051352280526
45784CB00007B/2924